Vistas of History

Samuel Eliot Morison receiving the diploma of the Balzan Award at the Quirinal, May 11, 1963. President Segni, wearing his insignia as Grand Master of the Order of Merit, is in the center. Professor Arangio-Ruiz is behind Morison.

Vistas *of* History

Samuel Eliot Morison

New York Alfred · A · Knopf

1 9 6 4

L. C. catalog card number: 64–19085

"Life in the 'Old Colony' in the Seventeenth Century" first appeared as Chapters XVI, XVII, and XVIII in *The Story of the "Old Colony" of New Plymouth* by Samuel Eliot Morison, published by Alfred A. Knopf, Inc., in 1956.

"The Wisdom of Benjamin Franklin" appeared originally in *The Saturday Evening Post*.

"The Peace Convention of February 1861" is reprinted from *The Massachusetts Historical Society Proceedings*, Volume 73, with permission.

"The Battle off Samar" is reprinted from *The Two-Ocean War* by Samuel Eliot Morison, by permission of Little, Brown and Co.–Atlantic Monthly Press.

FOR

Priscilla Barton Morison

BELOVED COMPANION BOTH IN TRIUMPH
AND IN TRIBULATION

FOREWORD

Signor Eugenio Balzan, one of the editors of the famous *Corriere della Sera* of Milan, unable to accept Mussolini's tyranny, chose to leave his country, and its Fascist regime, and settle in Zürich. There, through finance and investment banking, he amassed a considerable fortune, which he bequeathed to his daughter Angela Lina, with the request that in her will she establish a foundation to provide a prize for peace and awards for achievement in the arts and sciences. Signora Angela, after duly observing her father's wishes, died a few years ago. Under her will the Fondation Internationale Balzan was created, with headquarters at Zürich, Milan, and Rome. The Executive Committee has two honorary presidents, the President of the Italian Republic and the President of the Swiss Confederation, and consists of many Italian and Swiss gentlemen and one lady, all of whom were appointed by Angela Lina Balzan. There is a General Committee on Prizes, consisting of thirty-five members, of which Giovanni Gronchi, former President of the Italian Republic, has the title of First President; the executive president was Professor Vincenzo

Arangio-Ruiz of the Faculty of Law, University of Rome. This committee, representing many disciplines and every part of the globe, decides what subjects will be awarded each year and, after consulting special *ad hoc* committees, to whom they are to be given.

Since organizing the Fondation Internationale Balzan required considerable time and effort, the Prize Committee in 1962 made the unique award of the peace prize, which was given to the Nobel Foundation; and this addition to the Nobel endowment has enabled that foundation to equal the Balzan award of 225,000 Swiss francs to each laureate.

For 1963 the Prize Committee decided to confer its first annual peace prize on Pope John XXIII and to award four other prizes for music, biology, mathematics, and history. Around March 1 the announcement was made that the music prize would go to Paul Hindemith, the biology award to Karl von Frisch of Vienna for his notable work on the communication system of bees, the mathematics prize to André Kolmogorov, premier statistician in the Soviet Union, and the history prize to me.

This was a most pleasant surprise. A colleague had told me that I was one among some fifty historians being "considered" for that award, but I gave it no more thought. The way I heard about it, on February 28, 1963, is amusing. The *Züricher Neuester Nachrichten* ordered its American correspondent to inform me and to try to find out what I had done to deserve the award. This enterprising journalist traced me to the Army and Navy Club in Washington, and told me over the telephone that I was one of five laureates, the principal one being John XXIII. The connection was poor, and two names reached me somewhat garbled; so when calling my wife in New York to tell her the good news, I said: "The Pope, Hindemith, Molotov, Povla Frisch the singer, and I have won Balzan awards!" To which she replied: "This must be a joke! Povla Frisch died years ago, and why should Molotov get a prize?"

However, a confirming cablegram arrived from Milan a few days later, together with an invitation to receive the award at Rome, in May. Owing to the Pope having been awarded the peace prize, the ceremonies were to be in Rome; and as that kind of thing is always done in a splendid and impressive manner by both Vatican and Quirinal, we were privileged to witness the pageantry that I have described in the first essay in this book.

The four laymen, as a small return for their awards, were asked each to deliver a lecture in Rome on his specialty, and three of us did; Hindemith, owing to his concert engagements, was unable to do so. My lecture, somewhat changed and amplified, is the second essay in this book.

This is followed by four specimens, as you might call them, of my writing, to enable a reader to judge whether the principles set forth in the lecture have been carried out in practice. They have been arranged in chronological order. The first, "Life in the 'Old Colony' in the Seventeenth Century," is a group of chapters from *The Story of the "Old Colony" of New Plymouth*, published by Alfred Knopf in 1956. This is a fair sample of what might be called cubic history—not exclusively political, social, economic, or cultural, but an attempt to co-ordinate all four aspects during a definite period in a specified area. *The Story of the "Old Colony"* was written as a juvenile, which accounts for the simple language and the emphasis on children; but it also happens to be the only available book covering the entire history of that colony.

"The Wisdom of Benjamin Franklin" is offered as an example of popular biographical treatment. As a lifelong student of Franklin, I was asked by my old friend Leonard W. Labaree to deliver a lecture at New Haven in 1960, when the first volumes of his new edition of Franklin's *Papers* appeared. It was first printed in *The Saturday Evening Post* of January 21, 1961.

"The Peace Convention of February 1861" is a subject which aroused my interest, when recently studying the Civil War, as one about which very little had been written. Delivered as a paper before the Massachusetts Historical Society in 1961, it is here presented as a limited and almost wholly political subject.

Since my reputation as an historian is largely based on naval and maritime history, we have reprinted (with the permission of Little, Brown & Company) a chapter from *The Two-Ocean War* (1963) on the Battle off Samar, one of the three separate actions in the great Battle for Leyte Gulf of October 25, 1944. This naval battle, to my way of thinking, was the most interesting and dramatic of the Second World War; full of surprises and stratagems, as well as an ever memorable example of the guts and gallantry of American sailormen.

So here, reader, I drop my anchor; and after you have heard the rumble of the chain cable through the hawse-hole, and the officer of the deck has let out sufficient scope, you may ride snug and, I hope, enjoy what Alfred Knopf and I have to offer.

S.E.M.

Northeast Harbor, Maine
All Souls' Day 1963

CONTENTS

ILLUSTRATIONS

Vistas of History

CHAPTER I Receiving the Balzan Award

ﾞ

Priscilla and I arrived in Rome on the first day of May; but, apart from a delightful dinner with Professor Arangio-Ruiz and his wife and daughter (who had translated *The Growth of the American Republic* into Italian), the festivities did not begin for over a week. We went sight-seeing, the high point being a night visit to the illuminated Capitoline with the Mason Hammonds; and we made a memorable Sunday excursion to Subiaco. The Italian Navy was most attentive and hospitable; Admiral Giuriati giving us a lunch party at his quarters, to meet the Italian naval historians, and putting us up at the attractive new naval club. I was disappointed at having no opportunity to meet other Italian historians. One whom I admire, and with whom I ventured to suggest a meeting, was thus dismissed by the genial Arangio-Ruiz: "He doesn't want to see you—he thought *he* should have received the history award!" Possibly others had the same idea, which would explain why I met none outside the Italian Navy, where professional jealousy apparently does not exist.

3

On Thursday, May 9, came my lecture on "The Experiences and Principles of an Historian," the text of which follows this description. After it was over we were given lunch by Harold Parsons at George's, which we consider the best restaurant in Rome. That evening we stood in the receiving line with Ambassador and Mrs. Reinhardt at the American Embassy, the Villa Taverna, whose garden was illuminated with hurricane lamps for the occasion. The Reinhardts seemed to us to be the perfect ambassadorial couple: dignified, charming, and handsome. On succeeding nights there were similar receptions, which we attended, at the German Embassy for the Hindemiths and von Frisches, and at the Russian Embassy for André Kolmogorov. We thought that the American reception outshone them all.

Priscilla helped me immensely to carry everything off. Her ceremonial costume was a long black Bergdorf dinner gown with long sleeves spliced on by the Roman house of Carosa, which together with a black veil constituted Vatican court dress; for the ambassadorial reception Carosa made her a gown of royal blue embroidered all over, and the embroidery covered with blue beads and bugles. For the German afternoon reception she wore a black-and-white polka-dot dress with a black net hat, and at the Russian evening reception she appeared in a pale aqua crêpe gown with matching jacket, both by Bergdorf. All these enhanced her natural beauty, and each time she appeared the ambassadors and the admirals complimented her and congratulated me. Priscilla did her country proud.

Friday, the tenth of May, was the great day at the Vatican. Priscilla, after dressing all in black and I in Vatican full dress—white tie, tails, black vest, and wearing all the medals to which I was entitled—proceeded by car to the Grand Hotel rendezvous. There, as additional decoration, I received the massy gold medal and chain of the Balzan Foundation, but had to return it afterward so it could be *officially* presented by President Segni next day. This system was adopted by the Balzan Foundation in order to allow the maximum number of people to witness the ceremonies; and also, I suspect, to give occasion for double the number of speeches. Our departure was delayed at least half an hour by the tardiness of Signor Gronchi. That was unfortunate, as we could have used this time to better advantage at the Vatican than in the lobby of the Grand Hotel. Finally the procession started under motorcycle escort. We were fortunately seated with Professor and Madame Marrou, a charming and witty couple from Paris, who exchanged quips with us all the way.

At the Vatican we were taken in charge by Swiss Guards wearing their traditional uniform designed by Raphael, and conducted to the imposing Sala Regia, where, since the pontificate of Paul III, the popes have received crowned heads. It is decorated by paintings illustrating the history of the papacy, including the donations of Charlemagne, Otto I, and the King of the Lombards, doubtless designed to convey useful hints to royal visitors. Over the door to the Sistine Chapel is an immense fresco of the Battle of Lepanto by Vasari; I would dearly

5

have liked to examine it closely, but there was no opportunity. The papal throne was established against the north
wall, backed by paintings representing scenes of violence
which were in strange disaccord with the character of
John XXIII and the ceremony we were about to witness.
I afterward learned that they represented the assassina-
tion of Admiral Coligny, and Charles IX joyfully receiving the news thereof.

The Balzan and Italian state officials were placed on
the right of the papal throne, we four "laureates" in the
front row facing it, and the ladies parallel to a group of
about ten cardinals, among whom bearded Eugenio
Cardinal Tisserant and Gregorio Cardinal Agagianian
were conspicuous. A number of bishops and monsignori
were seated at right angles to us, facing the cardinals
and with the papal throne on their right. The Russian
laureate, André Kolmogorov, a very pleasant, gentlemanly
scholar who could pass as English, asked me: *"Qui sont
ces messieurs habillés en rouge?"* Paul Hindemith, short
and bald, and Karl von Frisch, scholarly and distinguished, with long gray hair that stood up straight, were
in the same row with me, all self-consciously wearing our
medals and chains. Every other man in the audience was
either in uniform or tails with white tie, wearing all the
decorations he could muster; the few ladies were in black
Vatican court dress with black veil or mantilla. Even the
privileged photographers, to our great amusement, wore
white ties and tails; but they behaved much like photographers elsewhere, squirming about and spoiling the view
for the audience in order to get good pictures for their
papers.

After a brief interval, a curtain to the door of the Sala Ducale was drawn back and Pope John XXIII entered the Sala Regia on foot, preceded by a colonel of the Swiss Guards. The colonel looked remarkably like a sixteenth-century *condottiere*, wearing beautifully chased armor with a white-plumed steel helmet, red velvet breeches, and red stockings. The Pope was escorted by a detachment of the Swiss Guard, also in steel corselets, and by some twenty members of his household. The clergy were in scarlet cassocks; the *cameriere con cappa e spada* (gentlemen chamberlains) wore seventeenth-century black costumes with gold embroidery on their tunics, starched ruffs about their necks, and swords, looking like Spanish gentlemen in El Greco's paintings.

The Pope walked to his throne. A young priest, in scarlet, kneeling, provided him with a footstool. On his right, throughout the ceremony, stood two prelates: the one on his right hand being his major-domo, Monsignor Callori di Vignale, tall, lean, and ascetic, wearing an habitual scowl, which suggested that he disapproved of the whole thing but probably reflected his anxiety over the Pope's health. Grim Monsignor Vignale, however, was offset by a smiling, plump, and rosy prelate on his right, Archbishop Venini, the Pope's privy almoner. On the left of the Pope stood Monsignor Nasalli Rocca di Corneliano, the *maestro di camera*, who acted as master of ceremonies, gesturing to the music (violins mostly) to start or cease. On his left stood Archbishop Van Lierde, the papal sacristan and Vicar-General for Vatican City; a tall, poker-faced priest in black cassock with purple trim, wearing an enormous pectoral cross. Helmeted, ruffed, and steel-

7

corseleted Swiss Guards carrying halberds lined the walls. One felt as if time had rolled back four or five centuries, and Julius II or Leo X were about to receive a state visit from François I or the Emperor Charles V.

The Pope wore a white woolen cassock, a red *cappa* trimmed with white fur, a white silk skullcap, and an embroidered stole depicting among other things two little one-masted ships, representing St. Peter's fishing vessel. The impression he gave was that of a benign father to all. He smiled frequently, broadly and benevolently, and in repose his face showed serenity and alert intelligence. He followed the long speeches with apparent interest, gesturing mildly with his hands and darting looks of approval from his eyes at references to the necessity for peace. Once, when the threatened horrors of modern warfare were referred to, he raised both hands and eyes to heaven.

Professor Arangio-Ruiz, president of the executive committee of the Balzan Foundation's committee on awards, addressed the Pope in Italian, outlining His Holiness's contributions to fraternity among men and nations, especially by inviting representatives of other Christian creeds to take part in the Ecumenical Council; and his tireless efforts toward maintaining peace among the nations. He mentioned by name the four secular laureates, graciously describing me as "historian of the American nation both in its formation and its development, and also, in the same field, an experimenter of genius, as is proved by his work on Christopher Columbus and his contribution to the American Navy in the Second World

War." President Frédéric Fouquet of the Swiss Senate then made a short but eloquent speech in French, referring to His Holiness's recent encyclical *Pacem in Terris*, and calling him *pastor et nauta* to Christendom, "which more than ever needs a good shepherd and a good navigator to compose its quarrels in a world so vulnerable to scientific discoveries."

After the speeches were concluded, President Segni of the Italian Republic approached the throne and presented the Pope with the Balzan chain and medal in a white leather case, making a brief address in which he adverted to the "profoundly Christian tradition and spirit" of the Italian nation, and expressed deep gratitude for the paternal solicitude which John XXIII had continually demonstrated for Italy. The Pope bowed in acknowledgment, handed the diploma and insignia to a monsignor, and from his throne delivered a short address in French. For text he chose I Timothy 1:17: "Now unto the King eternal, immortal, invisible, the only wise God, be honor and glory for ever and ever." He expressly received us, he said, "here in the Sala Regia, where kings and emperors had come to render homage to the successors of the humble fisherman of Galilee." He recalled how circumstances had changed, and that Leo XIII, on the occasion of issuing his encyclical *Rerum Novarum*, had here received deputations of workmen. "It is among them, humble sons of the people," said John XXIII, "that the aspiration for a just peace is particularly strong." He declared that this ceremony today "is the crown to a long process; and" (turning to President Segni) "by your hands a *témoignage*

9

of high significance is delivered to him who represents here below the Prince of Peace; your gesture translates, in the most eloquent manner, the unanimous aspiration of men and nations."

This is translated from the official report in *L'Osservatore Romano*; but I heard a particularly happy simile of the Pope's not recorded—that peace might well be "a bridge between heaven and earth."

At the conclusion of his address the Pope blessed the assembly; and with a charming smile remarked: "*Ça, c'est la* petite *bénédiction; maintenant, allons au Basilique pour la* grande *bénédiction.*" The procession re-formed, John XXIII blessing us as he passed, and all except the Russian kneeling to receive it.

Now the four laureates, rejoining their ladies, crossed the great square and entered St. Peter's by the west portal. The Basilica was aglow with floodlights, groups of candles on the great piers, and sunlight streaming through the Holy Ghost east window and the openings in the dome. Banks of seats, arranged on each side of the nave as for the Ecumenical Council, were crowded with invited guests—diplomats, high officials, and other distinguished people. The Balzan officials and the laureates marched up the nave under the critical inspection of the spectators and to the sound of the great organ playing voluntaries. The laureates were seated in the front row nearest the papal throne, and their ladies not far away. These were places of honor indeed, but not for the best view, as gentlemen chamberlains in black stood in front of us.

Presently there sounded a fanfare of silver trumpets as

the papal cortege entered the west portal, the Pope carried in his *sedes gestatoria* on the shoulders of the *bussolanti*, stout fellows garbed in jackets and knee breeches of crimson damask. They were preceded by gentlemen chamberlains in black, and followed by a detachment of the Swiss Guard in steel corselets and helmets, striped orange and blue breeches and stockings; the officers in gorgeously chased armor and white-plumed helmets. The procession advanced at a slow but dignified pace, the Pope smiling and distributing blessings as he passed; most of the congregation kneeling to receive his benediction. As he arrived at a point about halfway up the nave, the trumpets ceased to blare, and the Sistine choir broke out with Palestrina's gorgeous anthem "Tu Es Petrus." The Pope in his portable throne was gently placed under the great Bernini baldachino, below the center of the dome; and the Sistine choir sang *a cappella* Benno Ammann's anthem "Dona Nobis Pacem."

On either side of the Pope were ranged the same court officials as in the Sala Regia: the chubby, smiling Venini, the grim, ascetic Callori di Vignale, the *maestro di camera*, and the tall, black-surpliced Van Lierde. At the Pope's right, facing inward, were four benches of cardinals, including all those then in Rome; and on his left sat high officials of the Fondation Balzan, all in black, with members of the papal court in eighteenth-century costume of blue embroidered coat, white silk breeches and stockings, and sword. The Swiss Guard contingent, standing at ease and holding their halberds grounded, made lines from the papal dais to the openings of the north and south transepts; and the formal guardianship of the area under the dome was completed by members of the sword-bearing Noble Guard, uniformed in scarlet tunics with gold shoulder belts, plumed helmets, white breeches, and high black Wellington boots, complete with spurs.

The Sistine choir sang another anthem *a cappella.* Then came two long discourses, one in badly pronounced French by Signor Gronchi, the former Italian president; the other by a former president of the Swiss Confederation, in German. The Pope listened attentively and showed his interest by little movements of hands and eyes. Both speeches were discreetly applauded by the congregation. Signor Gronchi then re-presented the Balzan insignia to the Pope. He received them graciously, and they were removed by a chamberlain who on bended knee presented the Pope with his spectacles and a manuscript. From it John XXIII read an address in French, by far the most eloquent of the day.

He used as text the *Magnificat* (Luke 1:46–55). "The humble Pope who speaks to you," he said, "is fully aware of being small indeed before God. He can only humble himself, and thank the Lord who has so favored him, with a moving gratitude. . . . Glory to God, who in His goodness toward His servant, has given him daily the courage and serenity to follow his task in the service of humanity." In a bold and vivid simile, he compared Michelangelo's majestic dome overhead, resting on four great pilasters which in turn rest on solid rock (quoting Matthew 7:25), with the edifice of Peace, resting on the four pilasters of Truth, Justice, Charity, and Liberty, and

grounded on the Law of Nature. He then elaborated on
four verses of the *Magnificat*: "For He hath regarded the
lowliness of His handmaiden"—and "it is in humility that
the Pope who speaks to you intends to follow through
his action in the service of mankind and world peace."
The verse "For He that is mighty hath magnified me"
suggested the Pope's "lively satisfaction over the representatives of peoples lately entered into international or-
ganizations, to which they bring the enthusiasm of their
youth." Next, "His mercy is on them that fear Him
throughout all generations." No more revenge, bloody
rivalries, or recourse to force, "which humanity refuses
and the Christian conscience rejects with horror." Finally,
"He hath scattered the proud . . . He hath put down the
mighty from their seat"; words "heavy with condemnation
for those who separate themselves from the order willed
by God." The Pope recalled his earlier missions to Sofia,
Istanbul, and Athens, and his patriarchate of Venice.
Then, after alluding to the door of pardon that opens
every quarter-century in St. Peter's he predicted that "the
luminous flame of peace will pursue its way, kindling joy
and reflecting light and grace in the heart of man world-
wide, making them discover beyond every frontier the
faces of friends and brothers."

The loud-speaker transmission was bad and I heard
little of the address, although nearer the Pope than most;
but it was enthusiastically applauded at the end.

The Sistine choir appropriately sang the *Magnificat* as
the procession re-formed in reverse order, the Pope borne
high in his *sedes gestatoria*, making the gesture of bene-

diction right and left, although his smile alone would have been a blessing. Swiss Guards and gentlemen chamberlains headed the procession, which was closed by about thirty members of the Noble Guard in columns of twos. They used a parade step which reminded me of that of the Grenadier Guards—each uplifted foot making a tiny shake before it was put down. As the procession approached the west portal, "the silver, snarling trumpets 'gan to chide," saluting the Pope as he left the Basilica.

These ceremonies must have been very fatiguing to John XXIII, although splendid and inspiring to us. He seemed to be in good health; there were no signs in his face or bearing of the illness that ended his blessed life within a month.

The laureates and their ladies now mingled with the diplomats and other spectators under the dome and left St. Peter's by a door in the north transept.

Saturday afternoon's ceremonial was civil, but equally impressive, and perhaps even more significant, since it was the first visit of a Pope to a President of the Italian Republic, and the second visit of a Pope to the Quirinal since 1870.

The laureates, again in formal evening dress with decorations, and their ladies in Vatican court costume, were taken by car to a side door of the Quirinal and ushered into one of the great state reception rooms, the Salone delle Feste, through corridors lined with the Life Guards. These are great strapping fellows at least six feet four inches tall, uniformed in blue tunics crisscrossed by white belts, white breeches, black patent-leather hip boots, Roman helmets with horsehair plumes, and armed with long, polished swords. Those in the Salone delle Feste stood at attention with uplifted swords during the entire ceremony.

This magnificent hall was set up for about five hundred guests, many of them Balzan or government officials, or representatives of academies and pontifical colleges and universities, and the entire diplomatic corps to both Quirinal and Vatican in full regalia. The Danish ambassador wore a dress coat and breeches of scarlet damask; the Dutch ambassador was in blue tail coat covered with gold lace, and long white breeches, and carried a plumed fore-and-aft hat; others were in dress suits covered with decorations. But the Honorable Mr. Reinhardt of the United States came in his dress suit undecorated, as American law prescribes. A Swiss senator was similarly appareled—"We too believe in republican simplicity," he said to me. The Indian ambassador wore the customary white jodhpurs and black congress coat; the Pakistani ambassador, widow of a leader of that country who had been assassinated, wore a Moslem version of the sari. She was short, brisk, and gave an impression of great intelligence. Several African diplomats were in native costumes, with sandals, which enhanced their dignity in comparison with those who imitated the European costume. About twenty-four cardinals and several bishops and monsignori were also present.

After an interval, during which a hidden orchestra

played three compositions by Vivaldi and one by laureate Hindemith (who when congratulated by me declared that he was displeased, on the ground that chamber music was unsuitable for the occasion), the laureates' citations were read and they were individually brought forward. Each was invested by President Segni (a lean, distinguished gentleman with white hair) with the chain and medal, while another official presented each with a framed diploma and a check on a Swiss bank for 225,000 Swiss francs. The photograph of my investiture shows several officials broadly smiling owing to a quip on my part: "I'm glad to get it back!"

Mr. Hindemith now read a prepared discourse of thanks in French on behalf of all four laureates. It continued so long that the officials managing the ceremonial were afraid that it would keep President Segni from meeting the Pope on time. Messages were coming in: "His Holiness has left Vatican City"—"He has reached the Palazzo Venetia," etc. So word was whispered to Hindemith to conclude. The musician raised one arm as if conducting an orchestra and said: "Just one minute, please!" then carried on for several minutes more.

Upon his conclusion President Segni, in full dress with decorations, left us on the double and arrived in time to greet the Pope properly at the front door of the Quirinal. John XXIII had driven thither from the Vatican in an open car through streets lined with cheering throngs and decorated with Italian, Roman, and Papal banners, and tapestries hung out of windows and over garden walls. (This, as it turned out, was the last time that the people

16

had an opportunity to see him in Rome.) He wore a red hat when driving, but in the Quirinal replaced it with a white silk skullcap. His vestments were similar to those that he wore in St. Peter's, plus the mozzetta and minus the stole. He still appeared to be in excellent health.

President and Pope, after showing themselves from a balcony to the crowd, and briefly halting for prayer in the Pauline Chapel, appeared at the entrance to the hall. Passing close to Priscilla and myself, they took their seats on the dais. The Pope again had his three flankers in red and one in black, the last-named poker-faced throughout the ceremony, and the glum Callori di Vignale looking, if anything, even grimmer. He was undoubtedly worried lest the Pope break down after being subjected to another long and tiring ceremony. President Segni made a speech in Italian and the ex-President of Switzerland gave one in German; the Pope replied in Italian.

Now the laureates were bidden to step forward and be introduced to His Holiness. Hindemith, who came first, told me that the Pope spoke briefly about his love of music. Kolmogorov, next, told John XXIII in French that he brought greetings from the people of Russia; and the Pope replied to the effect that he loved all mankind, not only those of his own flock. As Kolmogorov passed on, John XXIII took my hand, and I (taking cue from the Russian) mumbled something in French about bringing greetings from Boston, a city so Catholic that I expected mention of it to "ring a bell." But the Pope apparently took me for someone else, for he answered in Italian which I did not understand, mentioning a name that I failed to recognize.

I bowed and was about to release the Pope's hand and pass on, when President Segni whispered to him that I was "*il istorico della marina americana e de Cristoforo Colombo.*" At that His Holiness brightened up, put both his hands on mine, and said in French that, as each Pope had some particular group of men closest to his heart— Leo XIII, for instance, *les ouvriers*—so he especially loved the sailors, for which he used the Latin name *nautae*; hence he was very glad that a *nauta* had won the history award. I replied in French that I was proud as a *nauta* to share in his benediction of all seafaring folk. He gave me another benign smile and press of the hand, and turned to Karl von Frisch, the fourth laureate.

His personal greetings of the laureates over, the Pope left the chamber, walking beside President Segni and blessing everyone as he passed. Donna Laura Segni, one of the few ladies present, now came forward, singled out Priscilla, and shook hands with her, and her alone. The audience drifted into another great hall next to the Pauline Chapel, where we chatted with the diplomats and one another.

John XXIII impressed me as one of the very greatest men, in character, ability, and every human quality, whom I had ever met. In appearance he reminded me of my beloved grandfather Eliot, the idol of my boyhood; he had the same warm smile that is a blessing in itself, and the same twinkling, humorous eyes. And I hoped and felt that Priscilla's ancestors as well as mine knew about this high honor which had come to their descendants at the very center of Western Christendom, under the benediction of the most beloved Holy Father of our century.

Receiving the Balzan Award

Here is the text of the citation on my diploma, together with the distinguished signatories:

FONDATION INTERNATIONALE BALZAN

PRIX BALZAN pour L'HISTOIRE—1962

A

SAMUEL ELIOT MORISON

Pour la valeur exemplaire d'une oeuvre étendue sur près d'un demi siècle, — Pour le mérite technique des nombreux travaux qu'il a consacrés à l'histoire maritime des États-Unis, — Pour l'étendue de sa curiosité et cette capacité de comprehension qui lui ont permis par exemple de fair revivre la grande personnalité d'un Christophe Colomb, — Pour la rigueur de son esprit critique et la sûreté de son jugement qui ont permis à cet historien de la marine américaine, pendant la IIe guerre mondiale, de rechercher le témoignage des anciens adversaires de sa nation et d'accueillir avec impartialité leur point de vue, — Pour ses talents d'écrivain qui lui ont permis de communiquer son savoir dans les livres, dont on peut dire qu'ils constituent une contribution, non seulement à l'avancement de la science, mais aussi à l'enrichissement de la culture contemporaine.

Le Président Executif   Le Premier Président
Du Comité Général des Prix   Du Comité Général des Prix
VINCENZO ARANGIO-RUIZ   GIOVANNI GRONCHI

Les Présidents d'Honneur
ANTONIO SEGNI   WILLY SPÜHLER

ZURICH le 1er Mars 1963; ROME le 10 Mai 1963[1]

---

[1] The diploma is dated 1962, when the award was voted, but it was signed in 1963.

CHAPTER II The Experiences and

Principles of an Historian

The high and signal honor that the Fondation Internationale Balzan has conferred on me, creates an obligation
to tell something of my life as an historian. During
forty years as an active professor of history, I never attempted to analyze my historical methods, or even to
lecture on it to my students. Consequently, this discourse
is somewhat of a trial autobiography. Historical biography,
which is only history in a special framework, is to be
understood as included.

Since studying under masters such as Haskins and
Channing at Harvard and Vandal and Seignobos in Paris,
I have been a disciple of the now unpopular principle of
Ranke, that history should be told *wie es eigentlich ist
gewesen*—as it actually happened. Thucydides stated it
even better in his *Peloponnesian War*, written some 2200
years earlier: "The absence of romance in my history will,
I fear, detract somewhat from its interest. But if he who
desires to have before his eyes a true picture of the events
which have occurred, and of like events which may be

expected to occur hereafter . . . shall pronounce what I have written to be useful, then I shall be satisfied." That well sums up what little philosophy of history I profess. I belong to no school, neither liberal nor reactionary, neither tragic nor romantic, neither deterministic nor cyclical. I simply try to write "a true picture of the events which have occurred." But it is my constant effort to do this with all available art, since without the writer's art no historian can connect with the public. As Professor Marrou writes: *"Pour mener à bien sa tâche, pour remplir vraiment sa fonction, il est nécessaire que l'historien soit aussi un grand écrivain."*[1]

Italy well names history *storia*, for history is primarily the story of man. Even before writing was invented, the storyteller had to be able to hold an audience. His successor, the writer of prose history, sometimes finds it difficult even to reach an audience. Sir Winston Churchill declared, in one of his less optimistic moments: "History with its flickering lamp, stumbles along the trail of the past, trying to reconstruct its scenes, to revive its echoes, and kindle with pale gleams the passion of former days." But why must history's lamp flicker? Why let its light grow pale? Why should the historian stumble?

Similar questions I asked myself some fifty years ago, at a period when the art of historical writing in the Western world was at its nadir. During the nineteenth century, historians began for the first time to learn from novelists the arts of description, of stage-setting, of

[1] H. I. Marrou: *De la connaissance historique* (4th ed., 1959), p. 283.

character delineation. Sir Walter Scott in England, Dumas *père* and Stendhal in France, Manzoni in Italy, inspired such masters of historical prose as Prescott and Parkman in the United States, Carlyle, Macaulay, and the Trevelyans in England, Michelet and Augustin Thierry in France, and Guglielmo Ferrero in Italy. But, when I was a student, almost all writers in the grand manner were dead. Henry Adams, still alive but disappointed at the poor reception of his *History of the United States*, had retired, a disillusioned pessimist. Theodor Mommsen, the only professional historian ever to receive the Nobel Prize for literature, died immediately after—possibly from the shock.

These great historians were university alumni, but none had studied history in a university; all were self-trained; or, like Ferrero, approached history from another discipline. Yet the sort of history that young aspirants in American, British, and German universities were being urged to write at the dawn of the twentieth century, the model held up to them, was the German doctoral dissertation. At its best this mode was accurate, a contribution to knowledge, honest and thorough; but devoid of wit, color, or anything calculated to suggest that the past had been shot through with passion. Not that, like certain modern poets, historians had revolted against "vulgar intelligibility" and wrote obscurely on purpose. They simply knew no better, excusing themselves with such brassy assertions as "History speaks for itself" or "The facts tell the story." They were obsessed by *le fureur de l'inédit*—the craze to publish new facts, to present hitherto unknown documents. These books were written, for the most part, by scholars for other scholars; as such they served their purpose for a time but inevitably were superseded. Who reads Edward Augustus Freeman today? Who will read Sir Lewis Namier tomorrow? Yet people go on reading Freeman's despised "romantic" rival, James Anthony Froude, and also George Otto Trevelyan, the historian of the American Revolution whom Namier supposed he had slaughtered. The great public, when it reads history at all, takes it in the painless form of the historical novel or, at best, biography. And who will deny that Mr. Average Reader can obtain a better idea of Imperial Roman society from Robert Graves's *I, Claudius*, Thornton Wilder's *Ides of March*, and Marguerite Yourcenar's *Hadrian's Diary*, than from the monumental work of Mommsen?

In order to restore Clio to her once high estate as not least of the Muses, her devotees must do something besides print documents, dig out facts and marshal them in sober prose; they must write in three dimensions, as it were, drawing not only on records but on their own experience and background knowledge, to re-create the past. An historian should yield himself to his subject, become immersed in the place and period of his choice, standing apart from it now and then for a fresh view; as a navigator, after taking soundings off a strange coast, retires to peruse his charts and then emerges to give the necessary orders to continue the voyage safely. And I would add that it is even more important now than in 1901 to write history in three dimensions because the background, the common knowledge that one could assume in 1901, has slipped away, driven out by the internal-combustion engine, nuclear fission, and Dr. Freud.

Gone is the classical education shared by most of the reading public sixty years ago; almost gone are the subtleties of theological disputation; gone is the economy based on the small, close-built town, the peasant farm, the horse, and the sailing ship. You cannot assume that any reader of the rising generation would know who Cato the Censor was, or could grasp a reference to a harrow, or would regard spending a whole day in the forest, felling trees with an ax, as anything but a waste of time, or could imagine why there should have been such a to-do between Luther and Calvin—although they will take great pains to understand why Mao quarrels with Khrushchev. As for the Freudian influence, an American wit remarked that Psalm 23, "The Lord is my shepherd," should now read: "A psychiatrist is my shepherd, he leadeth me to green couches!" This vast change in man's environment and intellectual interests during the last sixty years poses a new challenge to the historian. If someone should try to rewrite history in the light of Freud, nuclear fission, and an assumed collapse of democracy, I wish him well. But if he is bent on explaining past ages to modern youth, he must attempt to describe the economic and social order which in those ages flourished, and eventually faded into something else.

For me, the greatest economic-social historian was the late R. H. Tawney. That man of genius made a great book out of dull facts and refractory material. His *Religion and the Rise of Capitalism* (1926) was rejected by the publisher to whom it was first offered on the ground that nobody would wish to read a book on that subject. But the more discerning publisher who accepted it reaped a harvest because of the keenness of Tawney's perception and the magic of his style.

Tawney, who died in 1962, came too late for me to look up to as a young man, though I later profited by his lectures at Oxford. Earlier, when looking about for a model or inspiration, even Gibbon did not satisfy me; his Romans behaved too much like eighteenth-century Englishmen. After reading Burckhardt, who seemed pedantic and opinionated, and the hopelessly romantic Michelet, I came to Guglielmo Ferrero. He was widely read by American students in my college days, although our masters warned us against him as tendentious and tried to persuade us to read Mommsen instead. Ferrero taught me the importance of social history—of things like wine and song that the German historians ignored, and the "hidden forces" which were his delight to root out and display. And he had just enough dialectical materialism to excite young men who were playing socialist. Had I intended to be an historian of the ancient world, Ferrero would undoubtedly have been my model. But, as my ambition was to be an historian of my own country and the modern world, I found my inspiration just around the corner, as it were, in my grandfather's friend Francis Parkman, the North American historian whose fifteen or more volumes on France in the New World were written between 1851 and 1893.

Parkman was a man of the outdoors, an accomplished horseman, fisherman, and hunter, a lover of the great northern forest that covered most of Canada and the United States during their colonial period. He wrote about the long conflict between the French, the English, and the red Indians, not as a scholar in a nineteenth-century library, but as a participant. He obeyed the dictum of Polybius that the historian should be a man of action. Parkman visited every scene of the actions he describes; he sojourned in the forest, living only on the fish he could catch and the game that he killed; he shot rapids in birch-bark canoes with Indian guides; he even joined a band of Sioux Indians in the Far West, and from that intimacy learned to know the savages as they were, discarding Rousseau's sentimental conception of them. On a youthful visit to Rome he even joined a retreat at the Monastery of the Passionist Fathers in order to gain knowledge of the Roman Catholic; for as son of a Protestant clergyman in Boston he realized full well that that side of his education had been neglected. But he also made as rigorous and thorough a research as any Ph.D. in the archives of France, Canada, and England. His histories not only are so well documented that seldom can any critic find his facts at fault; they also breathe the aroma of the forest and the wilderness trail, they re-create the atmosphere in which his characters live and move, so that the reader has a sense of participation in the drama of a great nation conquering the wilderness. Parkman's works have endured; and why they have endured is best told by one of his Canadian admirers, M. Fauteux, at the centenary of his birth in 1923:

The Experiences and Principles of an Historian

Si Parkman n'a pas vieilli, si les lauriers reverdissent sur sa tête avec un fraîcheur toujours nouvelle, c'est que son oeuvre est jeune de la jeunesse immortelle de l'art. Tout en ne négligeant rien de la méthode scientifique, sans laquelle l'historien risquerait de manquer au premier de ses devoirs, l'exactitude; ... il a superposé la magie du style. L'érudit se double chez lui d'un artiste. Toute son histoire est traversée d'un large souffle qui la soutient et qui l'anime: le don de vie.

That is it—art and vitality. Parkman's work is forever young, "with the immortal youth of art"; his men and women are alive; they feel, think, and act within the framework of a living nature. In Parkman's prose the forests ever murmur, the rapids perpetually foam and roar; the people have parts and passions. Like that "sylvan historian" on the Grecian urn, he caught the spirit of an age and fixed it for all time, "forever panting and forever young."

Parkman above all was a land man and a devotee of the forest; he had no interest in the sea, and after one transatlantic voyage under sail, which he found completely unpleasant, he visited Europe only by steamship, to study in the archives. Here was my opportunity. From earliest youth I have been an amateur sailor. My love of the sea, possibly inherited from remote ancestors in the old China trade, more likely acquired in the cool waters off the coast of New England, is so deep, almost passionate, that after my doctoral dissertation I turned to writing on aspects of history in which the ocean provides both basis and background. Hence my *Maritime History of Massachusetts*, my biographies of Columbus and John Paul Jones, and, above all, my history of the United States Navy in World War II.

In this choice I have enjoyed a certain advantage over historians such as Fortescue and Churchill, even over Ferrero and Parkman, who have written about land battles, forest forays, and military campaigns. For they, when visiting scenes of conflict, find the terrain so changed as to be almost unrecognizable; the battlefields of Waterloo and Gettysburg are so covered with monuments as to resemble great cemeteries; and those who would write on the development of the American Far West find the open cattle range cut up into farms, crisscrossed by railways and the American equivalent of the Italian *autostrada*. Imperial Rome, too, is o'erlaid by medieval Rome, Renaissance Rome, and now confused by the steel, concrete, and glass of modern Rome. (But I must say a word of praise to the city fathers who have made stringent regulations against altering the façades of ancient buildings, so that the essential appearance of Renaissance Rome is preserved.) In the last fifty years the bulldozer has done more to change the face of that part of the world inhabited by Europeans than any earlier device of man; and the bulldozer, followed by the skyscraper, has even invaded Asia and Africa. Henry Thoreau's Walden, the lake where he sojourned in Concord, Massachusetts, was little affected by the railway that traversed one of its shores in his day; then in 1960 a stupid, insensitive government, by sending bulldozers to create a recreation area, had almost ruined the scenery that Emerson and Thoreau loved, when a cry of anguish from America, Europe, and India halted the desecration.

But the ocean, like the starry firmament that hangs

over it, changeth not. Thus, when I came to write a biography of Christopher Columbus, I dealt with elements of sea, sky, and stars unchanged since his day. My knowledge of sailing enabled me to appreciate Columbus's problems and to evaluate his navigation. By following his voyages in a sailing vessel, I could accurately identify his landfalls, and the islands, bays, and promontories that he "discovered for Castile and for León," as his motto reads. Columbus was not only a great sailor; he enjoyed every moment of his voyages except when there was foul weather or threatened mutiny. On one occasion in his sea journal he remarks: *Que era plazer grande el gusto de las mañanas*—"What a great delight was the savor of the mornings!" That rings a bell in the heart of every sailor. For there is no beauty like that of dawn at sea, running before a tradewind; the paling stars, the rising sun kindling both clouds and sails rose color, the smell of dew drying on a wooden deck. Columbus was unique among early navigators in appreciating the beauty of seascapes and landscapes. The atmosphere on his first ocean crossing, he said, was "like April in Andalusia—the only thing wanting was the song of the nightingale."

"Romantic history!" some readers will exclaim, to which I reply: "No tags, please; read me first!" As in the world of poetry, so in the world of history, "romantic" has become a pejorative word. In several dull books about history and historians that have appeared of late, Parkman has been dismissed as a romantic, one who saw nothing in history but drama. Now, if Parkman be a romantic, I shall be proud to be painted with the same brush; but

Parkman saw plenty of things in history besides drama. In his *Old Regime in Canada* he has chapters on Marriage and Population, Trade and Industry, Priests and People, Morals and Manners, that are models of social and economic history.[2] The story of Columbus is dramatic indeed; but besides relating the story of his voyages I made a point of describing how a ship was sailed and navigated, and how people spent their time at sea on voyages that might extend into months. Romance is a part of life, and it will be a sorry era that yields no drama to the questing historian. What Thucydides apparently meant by "absence of romance" in the passage quoted at the beginning of this essay was absence of love interest, to which his readers were accustomed in Homer and the dramatists. But romance, in the sense of drama, he has a-plenty; his *History of the Peloponnesian War* is as dramatic as a tragedy by Aeschylus.

My *Admiral of the Ocean Sea*, the product of several voyages under sail, and of years of study in the documentary sources, led directly into writing the history of the United States Navy in World War II. President Franklin D. Roosevelt, after reading possibly a few pages of the *Admiral*, accepted my proposal to be the Navy's historian, based on actual participation. This naval history, *une oeuvre de longue haleine*, of which the fifteenth and last volume was completed twenty years later, and a one-

---

[2] These chapters are reprinted in my *Parkman Reader* (Little, Brown & Company, 1955).

volume epitome in 1963, is generally regarded as my most important work. It was certainly the greatest challenge to me as an historian. It required not only a background in modern naval technique, but knowledge of infinite detail and the necessity to make a clear and coherent narrative out of a multitude of conflicting sources. It comprised a number of very controversial subjects, charged with emotion, such as responsibility for the calamitous surprise at Pearl Harbor, the Navy's unpreparedness to meet the assault of enemy submarines, and its bad thrashing at the hands of the Japanese off Savo Island.

At the beginning of my work on the naval history, I laid down certain conditions which the Navy accepted and has loyally respected: (1) I was not to be censored, or denied free criticism of officers; but on my part I agreed to respect security regulations, such as not divulging the nature of secret weapons, or printing coded messages literally. (2) I should not be required to publish until after the war was over, when I would have opportunity to study naval records on the enemy side, since military history written from one side only is worthless—the British Admiralty had to recall Sir Julian Corbett's volume on the Battle of Jutland, and employ Henry Newbolt to write another, because Sir Julian had ignored the German sources. (3) I could rove the seven seas in United States naval vessels, or work at naval bases, as seemed best. The Secretary of the Navy urged me to build up a staff, as most people in government service feel they must do, to make themselves important—"Parkinson's Law." But this offer I declined, having observed what happened to one of my masters, Robert M. Johnston. Appointed United States Army Historian in World War I, Johnston exhausted his strength and energy bucking the Army to build up a staff, and died at the age of fifty-three without accomplishing his mission. But I did have attached to me for short periods during the war several of my former pupils who were already in the Navy; and they, being familiar with my methods, participated in operations on one side of the world while I was on the other, and made extensive notes of their observations that were most helpful.

As my position in the Navy was unprecedented, I had to move warily and gingerly in order to obtain co-operation from those who were doing the fighting. Amusingly enough, their initial suspicions of a "long-haired professor in uniform" were dissolved by perusal of my *Admiral of the Ocean Sea*, which told them that I was a sailor before I became a professor, and thus exorcised the academic curse. So, thanks to Columbus, the Navy accepted me; and with many of its members I made warm friendships, which even survived what I felt obliged to write about some of their mistakes. But there were not many mistakes to chronicle. In general, our naval officers were highly competent, both in planning an amphibious operation which, if properly done, goes like clockwork, and in making quick decisions in a fluid tactical situation, the test of a great commander by land or by sea. Most of the mistakes made during the war by American naval officers were due to excess of zeal in coming to grips with the enemy, which, as Lord Nelson once remarked, is a pardonable kind of error.

In general, my method was to participate in an operation, then settle down at some naval base, read all the action reports I could obtain, write a preliminary draft, file it for future use, and then shove off on another operation. For instance, I first went to sea in the summer of 1942 in a destroyer, escorting a fast convoy from New York to the Clyde and back. After that firsthand view of this highly specialized branch of naval warfare, I joined the antisubmarine warfare unit of the Atlantic Fleet, studied the subject intensively, visited the principal training centers for antisubmarine officers and vessels, sailed on a patrol off the Atlantic coast, sent my first assistant on an air antisubmarine patrol, talked to hundreds of officers, and before the end of 1943 had written the first draft of what later became my Volume I, *The Battle of the Atlantic*. Next, cruiser *Brooklyn* took me into Operation "Torch," the invasion of North Africa by Anglo-American forces in November 1942, and returned me to Amphibious Force headquarters at Norfolk to write about it; this eventually became Volume II. In the spring of 1943 I went to the Pacific, in time to see the last phases of the Guadalcanal campaign; and so on, to the end.

One thing learned from this experience was the importance of oral testimony and visual observation. My history teachers tended to discount these and to put the document above everything as an historical source. In remote periods of history one naturally has to depend on inscriptions, coins, ruins, potsherds, and other artifacts for one's sources, and is lucky to have a papyrus by a contemporary. But the academic discipline of modern history has, I believe, placed too much stress on the very numer-

ous—in most cases too numerous—documents that exist,
forgetting that they are not facts in themselves but
symbols of facts; that everything in a document has passed
through a human brain. So why is a document superior
to evidence from the eyes, ears, and mind of an actual
participant? A human trait which naval officers share with
others is to rationalize decisions and maneuvers when
they write action reports; to imagine that they anticipated
all probable contingencies and directed the battle just as
it had been planned. But for a participating historian, it
often became clear that things did not run as smoothly as
they appeared in the official account, and that a victorious
issue of an operation owed more to the mistakes of the
enemy than to our own cleverness.

On the other hand, I learned that visual impressions
must be checked by documents. A good instance may be
adduced by the night Battle of Kolombangara in the
Solomons in July 1943. On the bridge with Admiral Ains-
worth, I distinctly saw three Japanese warships exploding
and burning. So we reported it; and the Admiral was
awarded the Navy Cross for his victory. But, after the war,
checking from Japanese records, we were disappointed to
find that we sank only one enemy ship. Our eyes had
deceived us. Our gunfire had whipsawed the Japanese
flagship so that her two halves looked like two vessels;
and what the third was, we cannot explain, unless it was
another Japanese ship firing so fast and furiously that in
the darkness her gun flashes looked like explosions.

After the war was over, I concentrated on rewriting
my initial drafts in the light of more oral testimony, the

34

numerous documents from our side, and those of the
enemy. It took seventeen more years to complete the job.
For some actions like the Battle of the Philippine Sea in
June 1944 and the Battle for Leyte Gulf in October, there
were six-foot stacks of reports by captains, admirals, air
group commanders on carriers, and others; together with
an enormous footage of documents from enemy sources
that had to be translated for me and worked through carefully, in order to ascertain what actually did happen. In
this work I was greatly assisted by two professional naval
officers, Captain James C. Shaw and Rear Admiral Bern
Anderson, who made up my staff after the war; and by
two others, Lieutenant Roger Pineau and Lieutenant
Philip Lundeberg, who were, respectively, my Japanese
and German language experts. Lundeberg had to work
through all the patrol reports of the German U-boats to
discover who sank what, when, and why. Expert assistance also came from Rear Admiral Richard W. Bates, who
wrote, for circulation only in the Navy, blow-by-blow
accounts of three great naval battles in the Pacific.

At the same time, I visited every scene of action in
which I had not personally participated; and in these visits
enjoyed the full co-operation of foreign navies, and of my
beloved wife. During the summer of 1953, numerous
Sicilians dwelling near the coast were puzzled by the
movements of a certain United States Navy motorcar
driven by a stalwart chief petty officer, with an Italian-
speaking naval lieutenant next to him. In the rear they
observed a young, beautiful, and auburn-haired American
lady, and her historian husband dimly visible behind

enormous binoculars. Mrs. Morison and the lieutenant, who between them could cope with any Sicilian dialect, frequently inquired the way to obscure beaches in which no tourist had ever shown interest. Whenever a crowd gathered, as it did at every stop, we interrogated all and sundry about the events of 1943. There was great excitement when our party debouched on a quay where Commandante Boido's smart *motosilurante* took us on board and put to sea in order to enable the historian to approach landing beaches from the proper direction. A few natives indicated by the Communist closed fist that they suspected something sinister; but the greater part were satisfied with the explanation that we were working for a navy that seems to have left only pleasant memories in Sicily. We shall never forget the kindness and courtesy with which we were everywhere received on Italian soil.

Besides helping me in this investigation, one of many that we made together, my wife has contributed to the quality of my work by listening to my presentation and criticizing it from the viewpoint of the non-military reader. You may be amused to learn that she has even played censor. When describing the tense, hushed mystery of a night amphibious assault on a darkened enemy shore, not knowing what might happen next, I proposed to quote that beautiful line from *La Traviata*:

Misterioso, misterioso altero

But she wouldn't let me; for, said she: "That means the mystery of love—don't desecrate it by applying it to war!"

From officers of both allied and former enemy navies

we received full and generous co-operation. Rear Admiral Fioravanzo made available the records of the Italian Navy; Capitaine de Navire Rostand and Médecin-en-chef Cras[3] opened those of the French Navy; Captain Stephen Roskill, R.N., and Commander Peter Kemp, R.N., did the same for those of our British ally. Several Japanese naval officers, notably Admiral Jisaburo Ozawa and Captain Toshikazu Ohmae, helped me to understand the movements, problems, and tactics of the Japanese Navy; Grossadmiral Karl Dönitz, Contradmiral Godt, his operations officer, and Dr. Jurgen Röhwer, historian of the German U-boats, elucidated many things in our vital war against the submarine. Officers of formerly enemy, now friendly, navies seemed eager to get at the truth and scorned to cover up mistakes. Naturally we did not always see eye to eye as to the interpretation of events, or whether a given decision was sound or otherwise.

So much for maritime history. There is another branch to which I devoted several years between the two world wars—intellectual history. After returning from Oxford in 1925, President Lowell, at my suggestion, appointed me historian of Harvard University for her tercentenary. This responsibility I gladly assumed because it opened an opportunity to study the history of ideas as expressed through academic institutions. It carried me back to medieval universities, Paris, Bologna, Oxford and Cam-

[3] Author of many works on French naval history, over the nom de plume Jacques Mordal.

3 7

bridge, and to the Netherlands universities, which the founders of Harvard imitated so far as their slender means would permit. It gave me an opportunity to study the lives and the ideas of English Puritans who founded New England and Harvard. Their interpretation of Christianity was not mine; but the more I learned of the Puritans, the more significant, even dramatic—"romantic," if you will!—they appeared. Puritanism as a form of religion lasted hardly four generations, and most of the sons of the Puritans today are either Catholics or liberal evangelical Christians. But the by-product of their efforts, the gospel of hard work, thrift, the feeling that every man was a significant factor in God's plan, created what is often called the Protestant Ethic in America; whilst the insistence on an educated clergy able to expound their Sacred Scriptures, and an educated laity able to read them, led to the English colonial emphasis on schooling and a free commerce in ideas. What has been more courageous in the history of education than the founding of Harvard, a college of liberal arts in a colony six years old, barely numbering twelve thousand people? Or more moving than the preservation of high standards in this college through infinite difficulties, with pioneer farmers contributing their bushels of corn and sixpences to maintain poor scholars?

My plan for the Harvard History included: (1) A volume on the different schools and disciplines from 1869 to 1929, each chapter written by a professor or dean who had lived through most of that period when Harvard evolved from a little brick college of the liberal arts to one of the world's greatest universities. This was a fortunate decision, for many of the data recorded in that volume would otherwise have perished with the authors. (2) A volume, *The Founding of Harvard College*, tracing its origins back to medieval Paris and recounting the early days of the little college on the Charles River. (3) A detailed history of the college in the seventeenth century; this was completed in two volumes. (4) A similar history for the eighteenth century. This last is the only part of the Tercentennial History, or indeed of any of my works, left "hanging in the bight"; but this period, and the nineteenth and twentieth centuries as well, have been covered in some fashion in my *Three Centuries of Harvard*, a single volume written for the general public. Taken as a whole, these books have set a high standard for American college and university histories because of their emphasis on the intellectual aspect rather than brick-and-mortar; so too for their descriptions of curricula and of undergraduate life and customs at different periods.

Editing a series of historical documents, or an old text, is a most useful by-task for any historian; it trains him in accuracy and pulls him into the basic materials. Three works of this kind engaged me for long periods of time, and none were financially profitable; but they gave me knowledge that could not be bought. One was *The Records of the Superior Court of the Massachusetts Bay Colony for 1671–1680*, which I edited jointly with the late Zechariah Chafee, Jr.[4] That taught me how the ordinary New Englanders really lived at that period. The second

4 *Publications of the Colonial Society of Massachusetts*, Vols. XXIX and XXX.

was a new edition of William Bradford's *Of Plymouth Plantation*. All earlier editions had been printed directly from the manuscript or transcript thereof, with all the odd capitalization, spelling, contractions, and the like which English writers used in the seventeenth century; thus few but scholars of that period could read them. In my edition, which Alfred Knopf published in 1953, I treated the text as if it were a play by Shakespeare—conforming spelling and punctuation to modern usage, but scrupulously respecting the words. Thus one of the great basic chronicles of American colonial history was revealed to a larger public. My third work of editing, which included translation from Spanish, Italian, and Latin, was *Journals and Other Documents on the Life and Voyages of Christopher Columbus*. Most of this work was done, with the help of Dr. Milton V. Anastos, when my *Admiral of the Ocean Sea* was being written, because all earlier translations were inaccurate; and, with the aid of several colleagues who were experts in botany and biology, the references to plants, birds, and fishes by Columbus and his shipmates were identified. This book was finally completed in 1963, and published by the Limited Editions Club of New York.

It is well for the historian to do original research when he is still young. It gives him the feeling of a discoverer to come upon something in a manuscript, inscription, or archaeological digging that nobody else has seen, or heeded, for a long, long time. Those ink spots on paper have been written, those lapidaries carved, those artifacts fashioned, by a sentient being; often simply as part of his day's work, but sometimes expressing ecstasy, anguish, or a sense of beauty and fitness. From the depths he seems to call to us to do him and his time justice; to understand how he and his people lived, and what they were trying to do. Through these records an historian, if he have art and comprehension, may let the light break through from a former age to his own; or, to state it in reverse, he may be a mirror reflecting the sun of high noon into the dark recesses of the past.

During most of the years my books were being written, war years alone excepted, I was a professor of American history at Harvard or Oxford, teaching undergraduates as well as holding seminars for graduate students. Except in my early years, when like other young American scholars I had to give nine to twelve lectures per week for thirty-six weeks each year, this teaching was no hardship. Lecturing to young men and women, or taking part with them in a classroom discussion, is a great assistance to one's prose style. The need to simplify, clarify, and impress youthful minds—even to hold their attention for fifty minutes—helps one to write. And those inconvenient questions that students are prone to ask, put you on your mettle to think problems through and come up with a clear answer. One must be intellectually honest; your young audience will detect anything false or pretentious sooner than the average reader.

Equally incumbent on an historical scholar, an obligation that he owes to the public, is the writing of textbooks for schools and colleges. Scholars do this more frequently in Europe than in America, because in America they are discouraged by the insistence of professional educators on dull, colorless compendia of history, rather than scholarly works expressed in simple terms. Notable exceptions to this lamentable standard are the ancient and modern histories by James H. Breasted and Carl Becker. Breasted's *Ancient Times: A History of the Early World*, which first appeared in 1916, not only presented the public with an adequate account of ancient civilizations prior to that of Greece; it was written in a fascinating style. My wife tells me that when she was so fortunate as to have Breasted for a textbook in her school in Baltimore, she could not resist reading ahead of the daily assignments, to the damage of her grades in mathematics and other subjects! That is what every textbook in history should be like; yet few are. Henry Steele Commager and I flatter ourselves that our two-volume *Growth of the American Republic*, which during thirty years has required five editions and has been translated into Italian, German, Spanish, and Portuguese, is a textbook of literary value. And I should dearly love to cap my career with a textbook on American history written especially for high-school students; one which they would enjoy reading and which would lead them to love their country's past instead of considering it a bore—the result of lame teaching and foot-dragging texts.

In my time I have witnessed the rise and fall of several alleged new methods of teaching history to the young. At one time the progressive craze was to teach "trends," not facts; that has now gone. Any method seems to succeed in attracting students' interest if it is conducted by an intelligent and enthusiastic teacher who has taken part in working out details of the system; but after it gets into

the hands of less skilled or interested teachers, it is apt
to get out of hand or become routine, and replaced by the
conventional textbook. There has recently been called to
my attention a new method worked out by Educational
Services, Incorporated, a group of M.I.T. and Harvard
professors who have reorganized the teaching of physics
and natural sciences in the nuclear fission age, and now
propose to try their hands at the social sciences. If I
understand the objectives of this group correctly—which
is not easy, as they write in "pedagese" idiom—they wish
school children twelve years old and up to study history
as a series of cases, which they call "situations," preceded
by the briefest of outline narratives; the materials for
each "situation" being copies of documents, pictures,
maps, etc., assembled "as loose pieces in a random pile
or bundle" from which the student is invited to select
what he wants. They have compiled a rather impressive
"bundle" on the formation of the American Revolutionary
Army in 1775–6, and tried it on a class of boys and girls
in a junior high school. I was amused to find that the
teacher who conducted this experiment—which took the
class about two hours a week for two or three months—
was disappointed because most of the students wished to
start by studying the narrative. "This could be dangerous,"
he reported, "as the unwillingness to depart from the
narrative tradition could lead to a widespread misuse of
this material when viewed from our 'Brunerian' frame of
reference."[5] My sympathies are with these children who

[5] The adjective refers to the psychologist Jerome S. Bruner, whose
book *The Process of Education* advocates teaching children almost any
subject by letting them arrange bits and pieces in a pattern for themselves. Since said bits and pieces must be preselected by some adult,

43

prefer the narrative. I believe that fourteen-year-olds would learn far more American history of that era—even from a psychologist's point of view—by reading selected parts of a classic narrative, such as G. O. Trevelyan's *American Revolution*, than by attempting to penetrate the mental processes of George III, George Washington, the House of Commons, and the Continental Congress through successive "bundles" of source material. This method may well prove to be one more aspect of that "permissiveness" which has undermined pedagogy in the United States.

My principles and methods of research and writing were largely worked out unconsciously, through listening to excellent teachers and following the best models. Giving "a true picture of the events which have occurred," as Thucydides said, should always be the historian's aim and cardinal principle; and, if he have the literary art "to bring it home" to his readers, "not only with conviction but with welcome to men's minds and bosoms,"[6] his writings, like those of Herodotus and Thucydides, may enjoy the glory of immortality. But merely presenting the truth with a modicum of literary skill is not enough; one must tell it with that balance and proportion which the French so admirably define as *mesure*. Observance of *mesure* will prevent overemphasis, in a general work, on

the process applied to history in high school does not seem to me to make much sense. As applied to theses, dissertations, or term papers, it has been practiced with great success in most American universities, for upperclassmen, during the last seventy-five years, although part of the discipline here is that of the student finding the sources for himself.

[6] John Fortescue: *The Writing of History* (1926), p. 72.

a single aspect of history such as the political, the social, or the military. *Mesure* requires the national historian to give credit to other nations for forces and ideas that have influenced his own; *mesure* impels him to do justice to movements and personalities that he instinctively dislikes, to try fairly to present what they were driving at, why they acted as they did, and not to assign ignoble or selfish motives to statesmen like Neville Chamberlain or James Buchanan, whose weakness or inherent amiability proved temporarily disastrous to their countries.

Tolerance, of course, can be overdone. The historian has both the right and the duty to make moral judgments. He should not attempt to prophesy, but he may offer cautions and issue warnings. I abhor the easy dialectical escape which would make a Hitler or a Stalin a mere puppet, the creature of blind forces, with no responsibility for his crimes. But even toward such men we should exercise Christian charity. The litany of the Anglican communion to which I belong declares: "From envy, hatred, and malice, and all uncharitableness, Good Lord, deliver us." These sins are particularly to be avoided by historians, notably in their attitude toward other members of their craft. Honest criticism is good, but the bad taste and worse temper with which certain contemporary English historians have been attacking one another is deplorable.

This brief statement of the principles that I believe every historian should follow leads me to something more personal, the means by which I have attempted to translate those principles into action.

Let me say here that, in spite of having received the

Balzan award, I do not rate myself in a class with those
great historians of the past whom I have mentioned. But
I do claim to be a good historical workman; talented, if
you like, but no genius. Such excellence in historical
writing as I have achieved has been in part due to a
fortunate background and great teachers, but mostly to
a painstaking cultivation of moderate abilities. As proof
of this, I was no precocious child, wrote nothing in college
days, and published nothing until approaching the age
of thirty. Good workmanship is my one claim for myself.

Hours of work, places for work, and the like I shall
pass over, because I have no regular hours but write when
I feel like it; and whilst certain desks or spots are favored
for writing, I can if necessary write in an airplane or a
ship at sea. More significant is the fact that the impulse
for all my books has come from within myself. The late
G. M. Trevelyan, a master of the historian's art, wrote:
"People will read history if it fascinates them. It is therefore the duty of historians . . . not to conceal its fascina-
tion under the heap of learning which ought to underlie
but not overwhelm written history."[7] To which I would
add, you cannot fascinate your readers unless you yourself
are in love with the subject. All my books were on subjects
about which I was keen to know more and which I wanted
to "tell the world" about. None were hack work ordered
by a publisher or the editor of a series. A wise publisher
will detect the light in a prospective author's eye when
discussing a subject close to his heart, and will figure that
the writer will do better on that than on something

[7] G. M. Trevelyan: *History and the Reader* (1945), p. 24.

initiated by him. And one good piece of advice I have for young aspirants in history is, if you have a strong desire to write a certain book, don't give it up. Two potential works on which I had done considerable research were renounced in favor of historians who felt that they had a prior claim. Then, to my great discontent, they never wrote them!

My next piece of advice is to do all research yourself, or through an expert assistant in whom you have confidence. In that respect I have been very fortunate. For the Harvard History I profited by the services of Dr. Clifford K. Shipton, now the director of the American Antiquarian Society; for Columbus, Dr. Milton Anastos, now professor of Byzantine theology at Dumbarton Oaks; and for the Jacksonian period in American history, Dr. Sidney V. James, Jr., now professor of history at the University of Oregon. Miss Antha E. Card went on what we call the "Old Colony safari," gathering choice items from the local records of Plymouth Plantation, for the history of that colony. For the Naval History I needed and obtained assistance, owing to the magnitude of the task, the multiplicity of sources, and the time element. Research for certain minor operations, submarine patrols, and the like was deputed to my assistants. But in writing most of these books and all of the others, I went directly to the sources, whether printed or in manuscript. A trained mind will see significant things in the sources that a young student or untrained researcher overlooks. Many facts and episodes dredged out of the documents, ignored by earlier writers who used the same sources, enlivened

The Maritime History of Massachusetts, Admiral of the Ocean Sea, and *John Paul Jones*.

Visiting, examining, and studying the spot where the event or events happened is indispensable. This not only gives you an authentic picture of the lay of the land or the aspect of the sea; but by letting nature put you in tune with the event, and giving your imagination scope to fill in the lacunae in the recorded sources, you may reconstruct the event. Since you cannot turn back the clock of history, as one can turn back the stars in a planetarium to any desired date, the next best thing is to visit the site of what you are writing about, and in imagination project yourself to the time and place.

Then there is the matter of note-taking. Students of history fifty years ago were advised by their professors, first to make a bibliography, and then to take research notes on cards or slips of uniform size (*fiches*, the French call them), not more than one fact to a card, exact reference on each. The student's skill was shown by the way he arranged these cards, by subject or chapter, and by the accuracy with which he quoted from them. My first book, *The Life and Letters of Harrison Gray Otis* (1913), the subject of my doctoral dissertation, was written that way, and it had only a moderate success. But in *Admiral of the Ocean Sea* and later works, pressure of time and circumstance forced me to abandon this system. For my Naval History, notes from personal observation, conversations, or documents seen on board ship, had to be taken consecutively in a pocket notebook, and each chapter was written directly from these notes and from action reports and oral testimony. I do not recommend this method to beginners writing their first book or to everyone; but I believe it to be the best for an experienced historian. Collectors of notes are too apt to get bogged down in them and to write dull monographs which are little more than notes strung along.

So, too, with microfilm. The young student with a grant-in-aid, coming upon rare books or a set of documents, loves to have them microfilmed instead of carefully reading and digesting them; that, he thinks, can be done later. Instead, he is in danger of becoming a mere collector of microfilm. Nothing is more pitiful than the student who gathers a closetful of those pesky little rolls and then does nothing with them. The career of Frederick J. Turner, a very great teacher who had the makings in him of a very great historian, is an awful warning to young aspirants. Turner became the prisoner of his cards and slips; he always had to collect more before he could write; and although his 1893 essay, *Significance of the Frontier in American History*, is a classic, he died some forty years later with almost nothing done on four or five books which he had contracted to write.

"There is the indispensable beauty in knowing how to get done," wrote Thomas Carlyle; that the collector of cards and film seldom does. But Carlyle always observed that beauty, notably in his *French Revolution*. Can you imagine that wonderful story of fire and passion being written out of a stack of cards? So, too, with Macaulay. Someone, Sir Charles Firth perhaps, analyzed a famous Macaulay chapter on the Siege of Londonderry and found that he used an enormous number of contemporary pamphlets and manuscripts. Since he did not try to convert these into slips, he was able to blend them into a narrative impeccable in accuracy and brilliant in style. Will Durant recently revealed in a newspaper interview that he and his wife write their monumental surveys of the successive ages by the card or slip system. After they have collected a few hundred or thousand slips, mostly (to judge from the result) out of books that other people have written on the subject, the whole Durant family sits around a table and sorts them. Then Mrs. Durant "processes" them. No wonder the result bears the same relation to history that "processed cheese" does to cheese. However, as the French say, "*Ça fait vivre des gens.*"

The unreadableness of the late Douglas S. Freeman's *George Washington* was probably caused by his excessive reliance on the research (very competent research, too) by others and his failure to pass that material through his mind before writing. As proof of this, the posthumous volume written by the researchers is as good as the earlier ones. In his *Robert E. Lee* and *Lee's Lieutenants*, on the contrary, Freeman did practically all the research himself, and wrote with a gusto and enthusiasm that makes these works live.

When I told the late Bernard Berenson that I was about to attempt a one-volume history of the United States, he advised me: "Write it in one swoop; then it may have literary value." My *Maritime History of Massachusetts* was written in one swoop, on a wave of euphoria; only eleven months, during half of which I was actively teaching, elapsed between the beginning of research and the finished copy. But I defy anyone, even "B.B.," to write a history of the United States "in one swoop." I have attempted to do it in a series of swoops, interspersed usually with work on other books—for I like to keep a major work and a minor one going at the same time. Taking one chapter or period, I soak myself in the sources, read or at least peruse the principal monographs, then sit down and write, always in longhand. Footnotes, if wanted, checking quotations for accuracy (a vitally necessary task), and all that so-called "scholarly apparatus," can be done later. After the first draft is written and typed, I work it over repeatedly and, more often than not, read other documents and books on the subject and introduce new material from them. Did you ever see a Yankee housewife make a piecrust? First she properly mixes the dough, then rolls it out, slapping it over and over; but in so doing she dubs in little bits of butter until it is the right consistency to bake. So, I take my first draft, written "at one swoop," dub in more facts, reflections, opinions, or conclusions, slap the paragraphs about, reject the irrelevant, read it to Priscilla for her astute criticism, have the whole retyped, and send it to the printer to be baked. Then, just as the old-time housewife may crimp the edges of the pie and cut slits in the top crust, so my last revision and smoothing up is done when the work is in proof, postponing as long as possible the final freezing of the prose in print. And even after the book is published, many things that might have been said better are discovered.

Old Horace had a phrase for this last process, in his

Ars Poetica: limae labor et mora, the labor and tedium of
the file; he adjures would-be poets to "curb" their manuscript for many days, guide it through many blots, then
pare it to the quick, like a fingernail. For a modern historian, his publisher will assist, if he does not require, that
paring process. Nobody is spared. I had to cut 20,000
words out of one volume of my Naval History. But I admit
that the volume was improved thereby.

My bills for corrections, over and above what the
publisher reluctantly assumes, roll up astronomically; the
typographical union must love me for the work created
for them; but no money is better spent than in getting
your writing *right*. For some obscure reason, a page looks
very different in typescript from what it does in longhand,
different in galley proof from what it does in typescript,
different in page proof from what it does in galley. At
every stage one detects fresh mistakes, contradictions,
infelicities of style, obscurities in meaning. William H.
Prescott and Winston Churchill had their first drafts set
up as page proof, and then rewrote them; but few today
can afford that luxury.

It is often difficult for even the most practiced historian
to write clearly what he wants to say—and, ironically, he
does not always know what he wants to say before he
begins to write! According to John Hall Wheelock, "Because a poet first learns what he wants to say by trying
to say it; the gradual working out of the poem itself is
what gives eventual definition to the more or less unde-
fined impulse that prompted it."[8] This is probably true

[8] *What Is Poetry?* (1963), p. 90.

of every art; certainly of writing history. Even if your ideas of what you want to say are nebulous, *start writing*, and the sky will clear, as fair weather always follows foul.

An historian must constantly keep in mind his expected public. On the one hand, he must soak himself in his subject and the period to which it belongs; on the other, he must continually be asking himself: How shall I tell this so that my readers will understand and enjoy it? This constant ambiguity, this dialogue as it were between the scholar and his audience, is one of the most fascinating aspects of writing history. But the historian must never forget that his duty is to tell the truth, as God gives him to see the truth; and that good workmanship is the basis of good history, as it is of almost everything else that human beings do.

Organization of one's time is almost as important as concentration. I have managed to arrange my work so that anything requiring a great library, or a certain archive, is done at that spot; rewriting, or work that requires a limited number of books, is done elsewhere. For instance, since the end of the last war I have gathered my library on Columbus and maritime history at our summer cottage in Northeast Harbor, Maine, and do practically all my writing on the period of discovery there, where it can be appropriately interspersed with sailing and other outdoor diversion. My secretary, Miss Card, looks up special points in the Harvard College Library. Research that requires the use of a great library I do in the winter, mostly in Boston, although frequent visits to the naval archives in Washington or Newport were necessary when the Naval History was being written. Trips to Europe, to examine the terrain of our military operations there, opened opportunities to do research on John Paul Jones in the Paris archives and to study early maps of America in Italian libraries.

Too many historical aspirants in America feel compelled, for financial or other reasons, to teach summer school; so that they have little time and less energy left for writing. Many years ago, Charles Jackson, professor of chemistry at Harvard, gave me a valuable piece of advice: "Sam, always take your summer vacation. Don't spend your summer teaching or researching. If you must have money, borrow it rather than teach summer school. My colleagues in the Chemistry Department all thought they had to spend the summer in their laboratories, to get on in their profession. I spent the summer cultivating my garden by the sea. Now they are all dead, but I am still enjoying my garden."

Down to World War II, when my children were growing up, I never worked in the summer, but enjoyed my vacation with them and returned to college in September in rugged health. But, as everyone discovers if he lives long enough, time becomes much more precious after the age of seventy because there is so little of it left. "At my back I always hear Time's wingèd chariot hurrying near." So, knowing that death will break my pen, I now work almost the year round, praying to be spared to write what is still in me to write.

Although my scholarly labors have not been slight, they have never excluded diversion and recreation. The importance of living the good life and keeping vigorous has always been before me; and to my wife's devotion and delightful companionship I give the credit that we can sail a boat or climb a mountain or enjoy travel together. Instrumental and vocal music, especially her singing, are a constant delight. The serenity which Professor Marrou at the Balzan award said was characteristic of my work could never have been attained, or retained, without a reasonable amount of play, a happy home life, and the Christian religion.

Advantages I certainly had in background and education, and a family which encouraged me to follow my bent. It was an advantage to be brought up in a city such as Boston, which fairly reeks with history, in a family which had taken part in historic events since the founding of the colonies and had pride in their nation and their city; to have been given an old-fashioned classical education with a foundation in ancient languages and enough modern languages to be used as tools; to have had as instructors the Harvard History Department of 1904–14, certainly the most distinguished group of historical scholars and teachers ever assembled on this continent; to be accepted as one of their junior members; and to have had congenial colleagues of my own age, such as Frederick Merk, William Langer, Robert Lord, and Arthur Schlesinger. Oxford, too, gave me much; especially perspective, conversation, and discussion. One of the great values of being on a university faculty is the opportunity to discuss one's work with colleagues. When the late Albert J. Beveridge, without any formal training, set about writing his magisterial biography of Chief Justice Marshall, he so valued discussion that he used to invade the study rooms of historians familiar with his field, and invite them to dinners where he tried out his ideas against their trained minds. An alert historian can catch words, phrases, even ideas, from conversation. For instance, the two concluding paragraphs to my *Admiral of the Ocean Sea* were suggested by a remark of Ellery Sedgwick when he read the manuscript: "Why, Columbus really had fun, didn't he!"

Faith in the Christian religion is one thing that "makes me tick." It may be conceit, but not (I hope) *hubris*, which makes me feel that in a small and humble way I am doing what God appointed me to do. In my twenties, having inherited a somewhat attenuated Puritan conscience, I thought it incumbent on me to take part in various "causes," sit on committees, teach night school to trade-unionists, etc. Oh, those boring evenings working out a housing code for Massachusetts that the legislature refused to adopt! Alas, those exhausting efforts to interest young plumbers and electricians in Andrew Jackson and Daniel Webster! There came a point where I laid my problems before my friend and father-confessor, the Rev. Smith O. Dexter, and he said (bless him!): "God has given you a great gift and vocation—concentrate on it, and don't wear yourself out working for good causes." Twice, however, I disregarded his advice and went all out for two lost causes—freeing Sacco and Vanzetti and opposing loyalty oaths for teachers. In neither case did I accomplish anything; but I was consoled by a friend's sending me that quotation from Addison's *Cato* which is said to have heartened Washington in the dark hours of the War of Independence:

> *'Tis not in mortals to command success*
> *But we'll do more, Sempronius, — we'll deserve it.*

As I look back over the years and observe the state of the world today, my last word to my fellow historians is to remind them that they are responsible both to man and to God. They must avoid exacerbating the angry passions of race and nation which threaten to destroy the world; and on the positive side they may help to prove that hate, greed, and pride have been destructive forces in human history. My hope is that some of our younger historians may prove to be instruments by which the brooding dread of our time may be dispelled, and a new and radiant era opened in human history.

CHAPTER III Life in the "Old Colony" in the Seventeenth Century

Introduction

The earlier chapters of the book from which this is taken retell the well-known story of the Pilgrim Fathers from the voyage of the *Mayflower* to about 1645, when the colonial boundaries were defined, an elected General Court or legislative-judicial body set up, and the economy evolved from a purely subsistence basis to cattle raising for the growing market in Massachusetts Bay. The chapters here reprinted attempt to relate how the people lived in mid-century.

New Plymouth was a small colony, even by seventeenth-century standards. A census of 1643 reported 634 "males able to bear arms, from 16 years old to 60," which meant a total population of about 2500, not counting Indians; it probably doubled in the next thirty years. After many vicissitudes, including a severe Indian war (King Philip's), New Plymouth was annexed to the Province of Massachusetts Bay in 1691. The transition was made without trouble or friction, since the laws and institutions of Massachusetts and Plymouth were very similar and the people were of the same stock. Among New England colonies, Massachusetts has long been the main target of dislike or object of admiration. It is true that some of the most enduring features of Puritanism, such as the town meeting, the free school, and the college, stem from the Bay rather than from little Plymouth. Yet today, when we look at our past for things to admire, we tend to overlook the proud and arrogant colony of Massachusetts and turn to her "problem child," Rhode Island, as the seedbed of religious liberty; or else to her modest elder sister, Plymouth, as a model of successful government under law and a symbol of faith and pioneer courage. For, after all, the Pilgrims came first; and for years they were alone. Their stout hearts won out, when there was nobody to help them.

1. *Local Government and Laws*

Whenever a new settlement in the Colony received recognition as a town, it sent representatives to the General Court at Plymouth and enjoyed local self-government. The local Freemen,[1] with other landowners, elected a board of selectmen, one or more constables, surveyors of

---

[1] This is what the voters were called. The first Freemen were the signers of the Mayflower Compact of 1620. They admitted others individually, but being a Freeman was regarded as a privilege, not a right. In 1643 there were 233 Freemen.

the highway, and other minor officials, subject to the approval of the General Court. Three counties were organized—Plymouth, Barnstable, and Bristol—in 1685, so as to provide courts of justice in three different centers. And each town had a selectmen's court which settled cases of damage and the like, provided no greater sum than forty shillings was involved.

Taxes in the Colony were incredibly light, according to modern standards, because there was no great wealth and the people did not expect much service from the government. Governor Bradford had no salary until 1639, when he was voted twenty pounds a year; and for many years more he had the privilege of dining the Assistants, when they met for judicial business, at his own expense. Of the other officials, only the town clerks, the Colony Secretary, who kept the records (for thirty-eight years he was Nathaniel Morton), the Colony Treasurer (Myles Standish for twelve years; then John Alden, Constant Southworth, and William Bradford, Jr.), were paid a salary. Every year the General Court decided how much money was needed to run the government and apportioned it among the several towns, which also raised local taxes for the church, the highways, and the school, if there was a school. Taxes were levied on real and personal estate, as today; and on "faculty," which meant a man's earning power if he were a merchant or professional man. Money was also raised by liquor licenses. There was no inheritance tax, sales tax, income tax, luxury tax, or any other of the innumerable burdens that we bear today. In time of great stress and expense, as in King Philip's War, the General Court increased the levies on the towns by several hundred per cent; but, unlike what happens today, they went back to normal after the emergency.

A strict Puritan Sabbath was maintained from sundown Saturday to sundown Sunday. Neither work, nor games, nor amusements were tolerated. Everyone had to attend divine worship morning and afternoon, and not go "sporting about the highways or fields." One Web Adey, for a second offense of working on the Sabbath, was "severely whipped."

All games of chance, such as cards and dice, were forbidden. There was no prohibition of drinking, but drunkenness was punished. The penalty was a five-shilling fine, plus sitting one hour in the stocks, for the first offense, double for the second, and triple for the third. And, lest there be any doubt about it, the law declared: "By drunkenness it is to be understood one that lisps or falters in his speech by reason of overmuch drink, or that staggers in his going, or that vomits."

There was little crime in Plymouth Colony; apart from petty offenses such as stealing, drunkenness, and idleness, it seems to have been a very law-abiding community. There were only five murders in the entire history of the Colony. John Billington, the persistent troublemaker among the *Mayflower* passengers, shot and killed a man in 1630 and was tried and sentenced to death. Governor Bradford, not sure that the Colony had the right to inflict capital punishment, consulted Governor Winthrop of Massachusetts Bay, who said, in effect: "Go ahead and hang him"; and hanged he was. In 1642 there was an outbreak of sexual crime among recent emigrants from England, which greatly disturbed Bradford and the Assistants; they wondered how "it could happen here." Bradford pondered the matter and recorded in his History three probable reasons for this crime wave: (1) The devil was trying to shame a godly colony. (2) If streams are dammed up, they break forth with more violence; so here, "wickedness being here more stopped by strict laws . . . it searches everywhere and at last breaks out where it gets vent." (3) Plymouth is no worse than any other English-speaking community, but all evil doings are rooted out and brought to light.

Since the Colony had passed no law against the particularly nasty crimes that had been committed, Governor Bradford consulted three ministers of Plymouth and Duxbury, asking, among other things, whether torture could be applied to an arrested man to extort a confession. They replied that it couldn't be done, since it was a maxim of the English Common Law that "nobody can be compelled to accuse himself." This is exactly the same civil right that has been placed in the famous Fifth Amendment to the Federal Constitution: "nor shall any person . . . be compelled in any criminal case to be a witness against himself." And Bradford followed the ministers' advice. Thus, an ancient liberty which has been sneered at and derided of late was respected in Plymouth over three hundred years earlier.

That case was unique; but, especially among the servant class, who were forbidden to marry until their terms of service were up, there were many violations of the

Christian code of sex relations. The offenders were punished by fines and by whipping, and by being forced to wear the scarlet letter, as Hawthorne described in his great story of that name. Sometimes, however, these immoralities were treated with a certain sense of humor. For instance, a Scots servant employed by the Taunton iron works seduced a young Irish married woman when her husband was absent. The court found the pair guilty, and the husband too, for leaving his young wife alone and "exposing her to temptation." So all three, husband, wife, and lover, sat in the stocks side by side.

For humanity, the Colony of New Plymouth was well in advance of that era. It never used torture, or burned criminals alive, or punished an alleged witch, or applied any of the cruel punishments which were then common in civilized countries. In fact, the Pilgrims loved their land so much that the worst punishment they could think of, short of death, was to order a criminal to get out and stay out!

Plymouth was no more tolerant of religious differences than any other European colony in America. The famous Roger Williams, whom Bradford described as "a man godly and zealous, having many precious parts but very unsettled in judgment," spent a few months at Plymouth in 1633, joined the Church, and was invited to preach; but he left voluntarily because the Church would not adopt his views. Bradford "blessed God" for having known Roger; but neither he nor the other Plymouth people wanted a piece of his "soul liberty." Samuel Gorton, who had the distinction of being expelled from four different colonies before founding his own at Warwick, Rhode Island, came to live with the Rev. Ralph Smith at Plymouth in 1638. After abusing his host and trying to start a revolt, he was deported.

In England during the 1640's the Puritans began to break up into several new sects, of which the most important were the Baptists and Quakers. Plymouth was not as much troubled by them as Massachusetts, because the ships from England discharged passengers at Boston. Its laws against religious dissenters were not nearly so severe as those of Massachusetts Bay. In 1649, the Bay Colony tried to prod Plymouth into cracking down on some Baptists in the town of Seekonk, but no action was taken. John Cooke, a *Mayflower* passenger, became a Baptist after he moved to Dartmouth in 1673; but he seems to have kept his standing as a local magistrate and deputy to the General Court.

Of all new sects, the Quakers were most offensive to regular Puritans, largely because a number of fanatics broke up divine service and "bawled out" ministers and magistrates in public. The first Quakers that appeared in the Colony stopped at Sandwich. Two of them in 1657 were called before the General Court, then presided over by Governor Thomas Prence, and questioned. One shouted out: "Tom, thou liest!" and another: "Thomas, thou art a malicious man—thy clamorous tongue I regard no more than the dust beneath my feet." Both were whipped and banished to Rhode Island, whence they wrote abusive letters to the Governor and to John Alden, whom they called a "self-conceited fool." Either before or just after this incident, the General Court passed a law against Quakers entering the Colony, and disfranchised any Freeman who joined them or entertained them. And all Quaker literature was ordered to be collected and brought to the magistrates to be burned. About ten Quakers in all were deported from Plymouth and five of these were well whipped before they left; but none were hanged or mutilated, as in the Bay Colony and in England.

The Colony was no respecter of persons; the worst case of religious persecution was directed against one of its most prominent citizens. In 1668, James Cudworth of Scituate, a Freeman, Assistant, and captain of the local militia, was indicted for "entertaining of Quakers to meet in his house." He was deprived of his military office and, when elected to the General Court by his fellow townspeople, was not allowed to take his seat. The Court of Assistants, having obtained possession of a letter of Cudworth's which was disrespectful to the Government and encouraging to the Quakers, disfranchised him altogether. One is glad to note that Governor Josiah Winslow, in 1674, got Cudworth readmitted Freeman and re-elected Assistant. And, being of a forgiving nature and no pacifist, Cudworth accepted a military command in King Philip's War when he was well over seventy years old.

For the most part, the "bark" of these anti-Quaker laws was worse than their "bite." As long as Quakers kept out of towns already settled, the authorities were satisfied; and by 1690 there were several Quaker Meetings (as their churches were called) along the Rhode Island border, at Rehoboth and Swansea, at Falmouth on Cape Cod, and at that part of Dartmouth which later became New Bedford.

Very few Anglicans emigrated to New Plymouth, and those that did worshipped in the Congregational churches and were admitted to the sacraments. There is no record of any Roman Catholic coming to the Colony to live, but in 1651 it entertained an important Catholic visitor, the Rev. Gabriel Druillettes, a Jesuit missionary priest from Canada. He came on a mission to New England in the hope of persuading the Confederation to declare war against the Mohawks. En route he called at the Plymouth Colony trading post on the Kennebec, then in charge of John Winslow, who had him as guest and treated him with respect and affection. Father Druillettes visited Boston and then went on to Plymouth, where he stayed with one of the leading citizens, William Paddy. Governor Bradford received him graciously and specially prepared for him a fish dinner on Friday, although Puritans rather made a point of *not* eating fish on Friday.

The Pilgrims were not political innovators, but we may claim two "firsts" for them. In May 1621, when Edward Winslow married the Widow White, they decided to adopt the Dutch practice of civil marriage. Couples were joined in wedlock by the Governor or one of the Assistants; never by a clergyman. The other innovation, a useful one that has spread throughout the United States, was to require that every deed to real estate be registered. The first colony in the New World to establish a registry of deeds was Plymouth, in 1636. And it was one of the first to require the registry of births, marriages, and deaths, which some American communities even failed to do in the twentieth century.

The Plymouth government was definitely a government under law. But there is little ground for reading into the laws and customs of Plymouth Colony the so-called "American Way of Life" of free enterprise and individual liberty. The Pilgrims were not interested in free enterprise; their ideal was the New Testament life, as they understood it from reading the Bible. Robert Cushman struck the keynote for the Colony in a discourse he delivered at Plymouth in 1621. The text, from I Corinthians 10:24, was: "Let no man seek his own, but . . . another's wealth." And, while he admitted that it was all right "for men to gather wealth," as Joseph did, a "godly and sincere Christian" should not do so at the expense of others.

Private property was indeed recognized and even encouraged, but its social duties and obligations were emphasized as they seldom were in the America of the nineteenth century.

Take, as an example, the grist mill, the first "public utility" of the Colony. A miller had to have a permit to set up a mill, since it affected other rights and properties such as the run of alewives. And when he had set it up, he was not allowed to charge "all the traffic would bear." Far from it! One "pottle" (two quarts) of corn was the legal toll for grinding a bushel.

And every other industry was regulated. John Jenney was given the right to make salt from sea water on Clark's Island in Plymouth Bay, but he was required to sell the salt for two shillings a bushel. Later, the Doty brothers and Thomas Hewes were given another "concession," to set up a fishing stage on Clark's Island. They could cut all the wood there that they needed, but they must not keep a dog, as the island was also being used as the town sheep pasture. Coopers were required to see that all barrels for salt meat, oil, beer, or cider had a capacity of thirty-one and a half gallons, and that tar barrels held fifteen gallons. The Pilgrims discovered early that tar for export could be made from knotty pine, not good enough for timber or firewood. And one year, after there had been overproduction, the General Court fixed a tar quota—no family could make over sixteen barrels of it that year.

Plymouth did not do much fixing of prices and wages, but those that it did fix were the maximum a man could take, not the minimum to which he was entitled. A man's wage was set at one shilling a day "and his dyett," or 1s. 6d. "without dyett," in 1638. Evidently this was found to be unenforceable, as it was repealed the next year, and the courts contented themselves with cracking down on "extortion." For instance, in 1643, some men who had mowing hay took "excessive wages, viz. three shillings per diem," and were told they would be fined if they didn't pay some of it back. Stephen Hopkins was fined for selling beer at twopence the quart "that was not worth a penny," and for overcharging on wine.

Price regulation was important, because almost all business was transacted, and taxes were payable, in kind. For instance, in 1674, the price of wheat was fixed at 6s. per bushel; rye or barley, 3s. 6d.; corn 3s., and butter 4d.

a pound, all delivered to the Treasurer, to pay taxes. Apparently eighteenpence (1s. 6d.) was considered the proper day's wage around mid-century. That was what soldiers were paid in King Philip's War.

A large part of the property now considered private belonged to a town or to the Colony in the seventeenth century. The Freemen of each Plymouth Colony town, acting as a land company, allotted (not sold) land to approved newcomers or young men who needed farms. It did not occur to them to make money out of the land. The spring run of alewives belonged to the community—and still does in the Old Colony and in certain Maine towns. At Plymouth, in 1663, William Wood and George Bonum were the committee in charge of "taking" the alewives when they swam up the brooks to the ponds. They must "let them go up on Friday night, on Saturday night and on the Lord's day," so that they would have a chance to spawn; and "take course for the preventing of boys, swine and doggs from annoying them in their coming up." They must distribute the catch equally among the townspeople, and for that service they were paid ninepence per thousand fish.

Cutting wood for winter fuel in the forest, which belonged to the town, was a community enterprise. Everyone who owned an ox team and sled was called out, and the men and big boys whose families had no oxen were allotted to those who did. Each gang chopped enough wood for a year's supply for all their families; and one gang who had shirked the year before were told that they must cut double this year. For it was a very serious thing for a family to run out of fuel during a New England winter.

Freedom of movement, too, was restricted. Nobody could leave town, buy land, and settle elsewhere in the Colony without permission from the authorities. A newcomer was on probation, as it were, for a year, before he could be admitted as an "inhabitant," and if he misbehaved during that year he was "warned out." In 1656, one Joseph Ramsden who "hath lived long in the woods, in an uncivil way, with his wife alone," was ordered to move to "some neighborhood" within four months; and if he did not comply, his house in the woods would be pulled down. For the Pilgrim ideal was that everyone should live in a village where the parson and constable could check up on sinners.

In Puritan ethics, the "waste of precious time" was a sin; one of their divines wrote: "An hour's idleness is as bad as an hour's drunkenness." This life was short; God had given every man just so much time, and he should "improve" it to his family's or the community's advantage. Massachusetts Bay, for instance, passed a law against "common coasters and unprofitable fowlers." There was no objection to real sportsmen shooting ducks, but the Colony did not want beachcombers and bad shots wasting time and powder, and scaring the wild fowl. For the same reason, Stephen Hopkins of Plymouth was fined forty shillings "for suffering servants and others to sit drinking in his house and to play at shuffle board." A servant's time belonged to his master; he of all people had no right to be idle.

The Plymouth Colony law on idleness provided that the grand-jurymen of every town must "take a speciall view and notice" of all people "that have smale meanes to mayntaine them and are suspected to live idely and loosely, and to require an account of them how they live." And, if they think proper, to present these idlers to the Court of Assistants, "that such course may be taken with them as in the wisdom of the Government shall be adjudged just and equal." And it was later enacted that these unprofitable citizens should be punished by "stocking and whipping."

It cannot be denied that Plymouth Colony had a "nosey," interfering sort of government that did its best to make everyone conform to what the Freemen conceived to be the New Testament way of life. Nothing like it is tolerated today, outside the totalitarian countries. But, unlike the situation in those countries, the laws of Plymouth were adopted by the body of the people, not imposed by a self-appointed governing class. And this was not exceptional for that era. We find the same sort of thing in the other New England colonies and in Virginia; and, except for the great stress on "no idleness," in French Canada, and in England itself.

Plymouth was not a democracy, in any modern sense. The Freemen were a minority of the men. The ex-servants who did well were often elected to town offices, or as deputies to the General Court; but almost never to high office. The principal exceptions were John Alden, the cooper, John Howland, who had been Governor Carver's servant, and Thomas Prence, son of a London coachmaker, who came over in the *Fortune* in 1622 at the age of twenty-one. The two Johns became Assistants to the Governor. Tom Prence showed a genius for marrying the right girl. His first wife was Patience Brewster, and his second the daughter of wealthy William Collier. That probably explains why Prence, rather than Alden, was chosen Governor for two years in the 1630's when Bradford refused to stand. And he filled the place well; it was said that he "had a countenance full of majesty, and therein as well as likewise was a terror to evil doers." After Bradford's death he was annually re-elected until his death in 1673, when he was succeeded by old Governor Winslow's son Josiah.

Josiah Winslow was in every respect a remarkable man. Born at Plymouth in 1629, he entered Harvard College, but did not graduate, probably because his father wished to send him on a voyage to England. His portrait, painted there in 1651, shows a sensitive and studious face; but he later showed excellent leadership in peace and in war. And he brought away from Cambridge something better than a diploma—the beautiful Penelope Pelham, daughter of the Harvard College treasurer.[2] An heiress, too, she made "Careswell," the Winslow mansion at Marshfield, a center of hospitality and culture. The Freemen, far from being jealous of all this, were delighted with the Winslows, approved their way of life, and annually re-elected Josiah their Governor until his death in 1680. He was succeeded by Thomas Hinckley of Barnstable, who had been an Assistant for many years.

[2] She was also great-niece to the Lord de la Warr (usually spelled Delaware) who was an early Governor of Virginia, and for whom the bay, the river, and the state are named. "Careswell" is still standing.

Thus, New Plymouth had only six Governors, including Carver, during the seventy-two years of its existence. And although between seven and ten Assistants were annually elected after 1634, only twenty new names appear on the list in over fifty years.

What if the Old Colony wasn't democratic? It had self-government, and government under law, which are far more important. The Bradfords, Winslows, Standishes, Aldens, Prences, Colliers, Hatherleys, Southworths, Brownes, and Hinckleys were a ruling class, an aristocracy in the real sense of that word; but they held office by the will of the Freemen. These men showed a judgment rare even among statesmen of great countries, when dealing with external enemies, internal sedition, and powerful neighbors of their own nation. The Freemen were very wise to elect them and re-elect them as long as they would serve.

2. *Houses and Clothing*

Around 1630, even before prosperity set in, the Pilgrims began to replace their early houses with more substantial structures. Thatched roofs were forbidden, and for the same reason—the fire risk—brick chimneys were substituted for the old ones of wood and clay. Brick, at first imported as ballast in ships, within a few years was being made at Plymouth.

The typical Plymouth Colony house from 1630 on was built of oak and pine around a great central chimney, and allowed to weather dark gray or brown—no paint was used outside, and little inside. The ground floor had two rooms, the "hall" (sometimes called parlor), which did duty as living room, dining room, and spare bedroom; and the kitchen. Each was warmed by a great open fireplace and was built low-studded to conserve heat in winter.[3] Up a small winding staircase were two "chambers," each with its open fireplace; and over them was the loft. The second story protruded over the first or ground story, not in order to pour boiling water on attacking Indians (as the myth runs), but because that was the English fashion of the day. The outside was covered with split cedar clapboard, and the inside sheathed with the same. Eel grass, marsh grass, or brick and mortar were packed between sheathing and clapboard, as an insulator. For windows, the oiled paper of the early days was now discarded in favor of imported casements with small, leaded, diamond-shaped panes. Heavy wool curtains were drawn over these windows to help keep out the cold. No square-paned sash windows were used in the seventeenth century. The floors, of wide pine boards, were scrubbed clean with beach sand. There were no rugs or carpets except a few bulrush mats made by the Indians. If anyone owned a "Turkey carpet," it was too valuable to throw on the floor, and was used as a table cover.

Every house had near it a barn and one or more sheds for keeping cattle, storing corn and hay, and for poultry or pigs. There was, of course, no plumbing, but every

[3] The Sparrow House on Summer Street, Plymouth, now headquarters of the Plymouth Potters, has a "hall" which well preserves the seventeenth-century atmosphere. And the Howland house is particularly interesting, since one half was built in the seventeenth and the other in the eighteenth century, illustrating the difference between the two manners of building.

house had its own well; some wells had a long well sweep (as may be seen at the "Old Oaken Bucket" house in Scituate); others had just a rope and bucket.

These houses were very sparsely furnished. Chairs, other than simple rush-bottomed ones without arms, were rare, and none were upholstered. Children seldom had a chance to sit on anything better than a stool or bench. There was always an oak or pine table in the hall, and a big one in the kitchen. Linen tablecloths were fairly common. Each fireplace had a pair of andirons; and the great one in the kitchen, on which all the cooking was done, was provided with a variety of cranes, brass and iron pots, pothooks, kettles, and skillets. Clothes were commonly kept in homemade pine chests. Only the wealthy had "court cupboards" of oak, which, in the next century, gave place to "chests of drawers."

Bedsteads were generally rough, homemade four-posters; only the wealthy had curtains and valances around them to keep out the night air. The Pilgrim who wanted a good rest had no better spring than a laced cord which was always going slack and had to be taken up. The most valuable possession in many families was a featherbed. This was a big linen bag stuffed with goose feathers that could be used either as a mattress or a blanket. Poorer people had what was called a flock bed, in which the stuffing was woolen rags and remnants; or a cat-tail bed. Most people had plenty of "ruggs" or woolen blankets, colored white, gray, blue, or green; and linen sheets, some white, some of brown "Hollands," and others colored. Everyone had pillows and linen pillowcases, which they called "pillowbeers."

Many of the dishes were wooden plates and platters, called "trenchers," but pewter ones were common, and a few people had earthenware. Wooden and pewter spoons were used, and there is occasional mention of an iron fork. That was probably for toasting, as table forks were very rare in the seventeenth century. You grabbed your meat with one hand, cut off morsels with your own knife, and ate with your fingers, wiping them, if you were very nice, on a linen napkin. Some families had pewter porringers for cooked cereals and soup. Very few—only six people who left wills before 1650—left silver, and that generally in the form of spoons, worth five shillings each. Bottles were usually of leather or pewter rather than glass, which was somewhat more rare in the Colony than silver. Every family had a big wooden "bucking tub" for laundry. Washing clothes was called bucking because the women slapped the soaking garments with wooden paddles. (Remember how the Merry Wives of Windsor hid John Falstaff in a buck basket?) Many families also had a "powdering tub" for salting down meat.

Every man owned several weapons, usually a musket and a fowling or "byrding" piece, a sword or a "cuttle-axe" (cutlass), and sometimes a rapier or a "culleever" (cleaver, or broadsword). Corselets (steel breastplates) and headpieces (helmets) are frequently mentioned.

These details are taken from inventories attached to wills prior to 1650. From the same reliable source we can confirm that the Pilgrims wore colorful clothes. How the notion arose that the men of Plymouth Colony always wore black suits and steeple-crowned black hats and carried a bell-mouthed blunderbuss that couldn't have hit an elephant at fifty yards' range, I do not know. Anyway, it is false. Puritans dressed like everyone else of their social class in England. Mostly middle-class people, they did not go in for the elaborate slashed breeches, fancy buttons, lace coats, and funny hats such as you see in portraits of Charles I and his courtiers. Nor could they afford them. But they wore no odd or peculiar garb, as the Quakers did. The only Pilgrim whose inventory shows many black clothes was Elder Brewster; and even he had a violet cloak, a blue cloth suit, a pair of green drawers, a lace cap, a red cap, a green waistcoat, and two green "ruggs."

Richard Langford, who died in 1633, had a complete suit of doublet, breeches, and cloak, a satin suit, a canvas suit (for working outdoors), a complete black suit, a red woolen lining for a doublet, a black hat and a white hat, a Monmouth cap (the usual stocking-cap headgear) and a "cap with silver lace on it," besides a pair of sky-blue garters and one silk garter. Will Wright, who died the same year, left a black coat, a blue coat, four waistcoats (one white cotton, one dimity, and two red), two silk caps, and one "sad colored" suit and cloak. These "sad colored" articles are perhaps what led people to suppose that all Pilgrims looked drab; but "sad," as they used it, meant simply a deep color. For instance, a "murrey" (mulberry-colored) red was sad; navy blue and forest green were sad, as were nut brown and orange yellow as distinct from pale brown and canary yellow.

The breeches worn by the Pilgrims were cut full,

somewhat like the "plus fours" that golfers used to wear, and were fastened below the knee by garters which had long tags called "points." They wore plain knitted stockings, or Irish stockings, which were really knitted leggings, having no foot but coming up over the thigh. Their shoes and boots were either of natural-colored tanned leather or black. Popular illustrators always place silver buckles on their shoes and hats; but not one is mentioned in a Plymouth Colony inventory.

A few Pilgrims, around 1630, still wore on dress occasions the stiff, starched neck ruffs that went out with King James; but most of them wore a "band," a large white linen collar that lay flat over the coat collar. All wore long-sleeved linen shirts, colored white, blue, brown, or green. Undershirts were then unknown; and though "drawers" figure in the inventories, they were probably light summer breeches rather than underwear. Cotton cloth came from India and was very expensive; only two or three women owned any.

The woman's or girl's dress of the period was an ankle-length gown, the bodice shaped to the figure and the skirt cut full. Under the laced bodice a "stomacher" was worn to provide a contrast in color or material; and sometimes a waistcoat over that for warmth. These waistcoats were usually red. For headwear women wore the coif, a white linen cap which came down over the ears, or a beaver felt hat similar to the men's; and, outdoors, a cloak with a hood. Their only underclothing was a petticoat, and a linen smock which fell below the knees.

The women's dress was even brighter than the men's.

A widow named Mary Ring, who died at Plymouth in 1631, shortly after her arrival from England, left a bewildering array of clothes and household utensils. She owned seven smocks; one red, one violet, and one "mingled-colored" petticoat; one white and two violet waistcoats; four stomachers; one black, one murrey, two white, and three blue aprons; white and blue stockings. She owned only two gowns, one of them black; but she left a large number of "peeces" of black, gray, red, and blue cloth, indicating that she was about to make up some new ones. Mrs. Ann Atwood, who died at Taunton about twenty years later, left a collection of six colored petticoats valued at £7 3s. 8d.; four of them were red, one of silk, and a green one made of a then fashionable silk-and-wool material called philip-and-cheney.

Children's clothes were of the same cut as those of grownups, except that small boys wore a long dress, called a coat, until about six years old. After that they dressed like little men.

Not much change in clothing was made for different seasons. People in those days expected to be cold in winter and hot in summer, and to get wet if they went out in rain or snow; waterproof clothing and shoes had not been invented. All children, and many grownups too, went barefoot in summer.

A word, too, on what the well-dressed Indian wore. He has suffered as much as the Pilgrims themselves at the hands of careless illustrators. Dear to the illustrators as the Pilgrim's black suit and plug hat is the full-feathered Sioux war bonnet (never worn east of the Mississippi) and a colored blanket draped like that of a football player on the sidelines. Actually the Wampanoags, and all Indian men with whom the Plymouth Colony came in contact, wore their hair in a sort of roach or crest from forehead to rear, and stuck in it a single jaunty eagle feather. They wore a breech clout of deerskin with a sort of square tail falling down behind; sometimes deerskin leggings, and moccasins on their feet.[4] In other words, they went almost naked except in cold weather, when they put on a mantle of deerskin to protect their chests. After they had been trading with the English, a woolen "matchcoat" resembling the modern mackinaw jacket was substituted for the deerskin. Women dressed their hair in various ways, and wore, as their principal garment, a deerskin draped about their waists like a Scots kilt, but coming below the knees. Young girls wore a jaunty little beaver coat; older squaws had to make do with deerskin. Both men and women, especially if people of rank, wore belts of wampum or of dyed porcupine quills as ornaments.

3. Manners and Customs

The same social distinctions that were observed in England and in other English colonies were followed at Plymouth. There was an upper class or gentry, a middle class, and a lower class of servants. Those who had been

[4] Cyrus E. Dallin's statue of Massasoit at Plymouth and Charles Hoffbauer's painting of Samoset appearing among the Pilgrims, at the hall of the New England Mutual Insurance Company on Boylston Street, Boston, are correct in every detail.

considered gentlemen and ladies in the Old World kept that status in Plymouth, and everyone elected Governor or Assistant, as well as the ministers and the better merchants, were regarded as members of that class. They were addressed as "Mister" or "Master" and "Mistress" so-and-so. Ordinary respectable folk were called "Goodman" this and "Goodwife" or "Goody" that; and servants were called by their first names, like children. The Pilgrims usually gave their children ordinary Christian names like John, William, James, Charles, Edward, Richard, Thomas, and Henry; and Mary, Ann, Ellen, Elizabeth, Alice, and Priscilla.[5] Old Testament names like Samuel and Ichabod were fairly common, but only a few parents followed the lead of extreme Puritans in England in giving such names as Desire, Resolved, Constant, Consider, Comfort, and Humility. Elder Brewster's two sons were named Love and Wrestling; the latter, generally pronounced "Rassle," probably earned its bearer a lot of fights. And we may be sure that Oceanus Hopkins and Peregrine White wished that their parents had been more considerate!

The family was the social unit in Plymouth Colony, as in England; and since there was always a shortage of women in the Colony, widows did not long stay single, and girls were married young. It was then unheard of, among respectable people, for the young to make their

[5] A poor man of Scituate, William Dennis, left three daughters named Remember, Dependence, and Experience. They had to split his only cow three ways. Mrs. Thomas Hinckley gave birth to a daughter who was baptized the very day that her father, the future Governor, was fighting the Narraganset Indians; she was named Reliance.

own matches. A law of the Colony made it a penal offense for a young man to propose to a girl or a maidservant without first obtaining the consent of her father or master. Arthur Howland, who found Elizabeth Prence fair to look upon, proposed and was accepted without asking her papa. He was haled before the Court of Assistants and fined five pounds for "disorderly and unrighteously endeavoring to obtain the affections" of Elizabeth. He had to promise "solemnly and seriously" that he would let her alone in future. We are pleased to relate that her father, the Governor, relented, and that the couple were married and "lived happily ever after."

Although some marriages were arranged by the parents, in most cases the young people fell in love and then did their best to get papa's consent. The marriage ceremony was very simple, without wedding dress, bridesmaids, or music. The Governor or an Assistant merely joined the couple's hands, asked if they took each other freely for wedded wife and husband, asked the parents if they approved, and then pronounced them man and wife.

No doubt there was plenty of romance in the Old Colony, but not much of that sort of thing gets into cold records. Everybody knows about the courtship of Myles Standish, but few have heard of the courtship of John Saffin. John came over from England in 1644, at the age of twelve, as a ward of Governor Edward Winslow, in whose house he grew up. At the age of twenty-one or -two, he fell in love with Martha Willet, who "in splendid beauty did much excell," as he wrote in one of his poems.

She was a daughter of Thomas Willet the fur trader, who by this time had become an Assistant of the Colony. Mr. Willet gave consent to the match on condition that John make some money first; and to help him, arranged that he should go to Virginia as a merchant.

Upon departing, John went to the Willet house to say good-by to his fiancée, but found her asleep and kissed her without waking her. So, en route to Virginia, he wrote a poem to Martha, of which these are a few of the lines:

> *Sweetly, my Dearest, I left thee asleep,*
> *Which silent parting made my heart to weep;*
> *Fain would I wake her, but Love did reply*
> *O wake her not, so sweetly let her lie.*
> *Thus in sad silence, I alone and mute,*
> *My lips bade thee farewell with a salute,*
> *And so went from thee. Turning back again*
> *I thought one kiss too little, then stole twain*
> *—And then another!*

John and Martha remained true to each other during his four-year absence in Virginia. Then, having made a modest fortune, he sailed home in one of those small two-masted vessels called a pinnace, to claim his bride. And, on the voyage, he wrote a charming poem, "To Her, Coming Home," of which the chorus runs:

> *Sail, gentle pinnace; Zepherus doth not fail*
> *With prosperous gales; sail, gentle pinnace, sail!*

Who could resist a young man who wrote such flattering love poetry? Anyway, Martha could not. They were married shortly after his return, and he continued to write poetry to her during the twenty years of their happy married life.

Most of these marriages were very fruitful; families of fourteen and more were common. And there are many tributes of affection in the wills. One Goodman Wright, who died at Plymouth in 1633, wrote in his will: "Whereas God of his great mercy and goodness . . . hath given me a faithful and loving wife which hath lived with me to the present time to our mutual joy and comfort; therefore my will is, and hereby I do freely give and bequeath to Priscilla Wright my loving and lawful wife, all real estate, livestock, goods and chattels." He asks her to give a ewe lamb to the Church within a year of his death, and to Elder Brewster a cloth suit which he had from Dr. Fuller, and five shillings to Governor Bradford for serving as the supervisor of his will. Priscilla is appointed his "full and sole executrix."

William Palmer of "Ducksburrow" had children living from his first marriage when he died in 1637, and little grandchildren too; but in his will he said: "Whereas I have married a young woman who is dear unto me I desire my executors to deal well with her," to give her one third at least of his estate, and one third more, if she is with child when he dies. This second wife, Elizabeth, had evidently been a servant, because her husband expressed a wish that she "should be ruled by her ancient master Edward Winslow in her marriage." And within a year she married John Willis.

William Gilson of Scituate, on his deathbed, told Edward Foster that he wished his wife Frances to be his sole executrix "and to take all that he hath and to pay all his debts." And when Foster suggested that he leave

"something more" to his cousin and servant John Damon
than his "land on the Third Cliff" which he had willed to
him, he said no; wife Frances should have everything
except that land; his aunt could look after John. Foster
himself died three years later, leaving everything to his
"loving wife Lettice." John Atwood, dying at Plymouth
in 1644, gave everything including "all those debts which
be due to me in Old England and Virginia" to his "loving
wife Anne"; and though he would like to give something
to his "little kinsman William Crowe" and his nephews
and nieces, he leaves them "to the will of my wife to deal
with them as shall seem good to her."

A custom that seems odd to us, though then common
in England, was to swap children for a year or more. The
Whites would send Johnny and Mary to live with the
Browns for a year, who sent their Dick and Ann to live
with the Whites; and sometimes these families lived at
great distances from each other. Dr. Fuller, for instance,
had a child from Lynn and another from Salem living
with him at Plymouth when he died, but his daughter
was in another family elsewhere. Apparently the motive
for this exchange was partly social, and partly the notion
that children would learn better manners and discipline
away from their fond parents.

Now, let us follow the day's routine for a typical
Plymouth family. The master and mistress, in their forties,
by this time have ten children aged from a few months
to eighteen years, and a young servant. The day starts
by one of the big boys or the servant raking out the wood
fire which was banked with ashes the night before, build-

ing it up again with pine kindling and hardwood logs, and bringing in buckets of water from the well. The mother, after dressing (and possibly washing) her littlest ones, comes down to cook breakfast. The favorite breakfast dish was hasty pudding (what we call corn-meal mush), boiled in a big iron pot and served with milk or molasses. The breakfast drink is cider, or milk for the children; no tea, coffee, or cocoa reached the Colony until the very end of the century. Breakfast is served at sunrise, or earlier in winter. The master of the house, after feeding the livestock, reads a chapter of the Bible and asks a blessing before anyone sits down.

Breakfast over, the mistress or one of the girls milks the cows; for it was assumed in the seventeenth century that cows would not "give" for men. The womenfolk also feed the chickens and cultivate the kitchen garden of herbs, "sallets," and a few flowers, which they call "posies." The master and the big boys go afield to plow, sow, cultivate, or reap; or, if it is winter, to the forest to cut wood or hunt deer. One boy has to lead the family's cattle to pasture (which is mostly woods), and to look out for the herd all day. Perhaps two of the boys are allowed to take the family boat and go fishing. Almost every family who lived on the coast went out after cod in the fall and "made" a quantity of dried fish.

Baking in the earliest days was done in outdoor ovens; but by 1660 most chimneys were built with a brick oven attached. This was filled with hot embers from the fire. After it was well heated the coals were raked out and the bread, pudding, or pot of beans was baked by the heat of the bricks. The common bread, called "rye and Injun," was baked from a mixture of corn meal, barley, and rye flour; for wheat never grew well in Plymouth. "Rye and Injun" resembled the brown bread which New England Yankees still like to serve with baked beans; but it was not so sweet, and more nutritious.

Dinner, between eleven o'clock and noon, starts with another blessing, followed by more hasty pudding. The main course is fresh or salt fish, beef or pork or mutton roasted on a spit before the open fire or made into a stew. Another mainstay was succotash, which the Indians taught the colonists to make. Colonial succotash was not the pallid side dish of canned corn and lima beans that is served under that name today, but was a meal in itself.[6]

For vegetables there were peas (picked ripe, not green), turnips, parsnips, onions, squash, and especially pumpkin. As an old ballad composed in the early days of the Colony puts it:

Instead of pottage and puddings and custards and pies,
Our pumpkins and parsnips are common supplies;
We have pumpkin at morning and pumpkin at noon;
If it was not for pumpkin we should be undoon.

Pumpkin was stewed, not made into pumpkin pie; the Pilgrims' only pies were meat pies. For dessert there would be an "Injun pudding" made of corn meal sweetened with molasses. And in season there were wild straw-

[6] The recipe furnished by an aged member of the Old Colony Historical Society calls for 2-lb. round steak cubed and boiled; 1 boiled chicken, 2 cups pea beans parboiled; 3 pints hulled corn cooked for 2 hours with the beans; 4 big potatoes diced and cooked with one diced turnip. Then you throw everything together, including the liquor in which the ingredients were boiled, and cook very slowly until blended.

berries, blueberries, raspberries, and blackberries; but the Pilgrims seem never to have used the cranberry, cultivation of which is now a leading industry in the Old Colony. The women knew how to preserve fresh fruit with sugar, in earthenware crocks sealed with wax; but sugar was so scarce and dear in those days that only the wealthier people could afford it. Molasses imported from the West Indies was the principal sweetening; maple sugar and honey were used, too. Nathaniel Tilden of Scituate left "10 stocks and swarms of bees" worth ten pounds, in 1641.

Dinner over, the men go out to the fields again or, if it is fall and the harvest has been gathered, to shoot wild fowl. The women and girls now set to churning the morning's cream into butter, or to spinning and weaving. Every householder was required to sow at least one square rod (a rod is sixteen and a half feet) of hemp or flax, from which yarn could be spun to make shirts and sheets. Wool was carded and spun into yarn from which stockings were knitted and cloth woven, if the family had a loom.[7] Dyestuffs were made from native plants or from imported materials such as indigo and cochineal. Some families evidently made cheese, as they had "cheesefatts," the wooden molds in which the curds were pressed.

Toward sundown the menfolk return, hungry for sup-

[7] This homespun and home-woven cloth was sleazy and stretched badly unless it was fulled, or finished, at a fulling mill. There the cloth was pounded with big hammers to a uniform thickness, and shrunk. A kind of clay called fuller's earth was applied to soak up the grease in the wool, and the nap was trimmed with big shears. James Torrey had a fulling mill at Scituate in 1653, and one was built on the Town Brook at Plymouth within twenty years. At the Harlow house in Plymouth, visitors can see the spinning and weaving on the old wheels and looms, done by an expert.

per; but first father must hear the younger children recite their A B C's and catechism. Supper is largely a repetition of breakfast, together with leftovers warmed up from dinner. A big pot of beans, first baked for Saturday-night supper, will do for Sunday as well. It is against Puritan principles to cook hot meals on the Sabbath or to do any work except to water and feed the stock; for Jesus Himself had said that that was all right (Luke 13:15).

Supper cleared away, a tallow candle is lighted and the master, mistress, and big boys and girls take long clay "churchwarden" pipes to "drink tobacco," as smoking was then called.[8] Maybe the master casts up accounts in a big book, writing with ink made of oak galls and a quill pen that was once a goose feather. Tales are told of the early days of hardship, of Indians, and of old wars. Members of other families drop in to exchange local gossip and retail such news as trickles through from the outside world; for there are no newspapers. Finally the master opens his great Bible, reads a chapter, and prays that God will protect them all from the "perils and dangers of the night." And so to bed. Father, mother, and one or two small children pile into the big four-poster; a little "truckle-bed" is pulled out from underneath for other small fry; there is a cradle for the baby; the big boys and girls and servants spread pallets of corn-husk mattresses on the floors of the other rooms.

[8] There is plenty of evidence that New England women smoked in the seventeenth century. For instance, there is a letter from the very respectable James Cudworth of Scituate stating that his wife was so feeble that "when she is up she cannot light a pipe of tobacco, but it must be lighted for her; and until she has taken two or three pipes, for want of breath she is not able to stir."

By the time a boy was ten years he had decided, with the help of his parents and older brothers, what his "calling" or business should be. If he seemed a likely "scoller," he was sent to the local minister for instruction and, in rare cases, went to college. William Bradford, Jr., Josiah Winslow, and Thomas Prence, Jr., entered Harvard in the 1640's—the first native-born Americans to enroll in the college—but no one of the three managed to graduate. Isaac Allerton, Jr., did graduate in 1650, but then went to live in Virginia, where he became a great swell. Very few Plymouth Colony boys, except ministers' sons who could be prepared at home by their fathers, attended college in the seventeenth century.

Many boys decided to stay at home and help their father until they married. Others hired themselves out in order to earn a little money to stock a farm of their own; and in a new settlement they could usually obtain fifty acres from the town, free. A boy handy with tools, or with a mechanical turn of mind, would be apprenticed at about the age of fourteen to a bricklayer, carpenter, ship or boat builder, or keeper of a grist mill or sawmill. He went to live with his master and worked for him without wages for seven years. Boys who yearned to go to sea would be taken as cabin boy or cook on a fishing vessel, coaster, or West Indies trader.

The girls were kept busy helping their mother in her household tasks, and learning to spin and weave and make butter and cheese. When they reached the age of eighteen they could choose between hiring out as a servant to another family or being married. The only occupation other than housewife open to women was that of midwife, to bring babies into the world. Elderly dames sometimes learned enough of the use of herbs and simple medicaments to become "herb doctors." They were called in whenever a child was sick, to administer a soothing draft of sassafras tea or maybe a purge. Practicing physicians were rare in the Colony, and medicine at best was so primitive in the seventeenth century that dozens of little children died of complaints that are easily cured today.

Servants owned no property, but were regarded as much members of the family as children. Often they were young relations sent out from England. Masters of families were required to feed, clothe, and shelter servants properly; the records are full of cases in which masters were punished for failure to do so, or for abusing a servant, such as requiring one "to bring a log beyond his strength." The head of a family was responsible for teaching his servants as well as his children to read, and for giving them elementary religious instruction out of the Westminster Shorter Catechism—fifty pages short!

Servants sometimes quarreled—Ned Doty and Ned Lester, servants of Stephen Hopkins, fought the only duel on record in the Colony. But in many families the servants felt brotherly affection for each other. John Cole, an ex-servant of William Collier, had very little to leave when he died. He bequeathed his bedding, clothes, and a sow to his brother; one sheep to his sister; half a crown (2s. 6d.) each "unto Master Collier's men, namely Edward, Joseph, Arthur, Ralph and John," and five shillings to his master's daughter Elizabeth. The Colliers must indeed have been a happy family.

Menservants who had behaved themselves were always given a tract of land by a town when their terms of service expired. Many servants, however, were unruly and lazy, and such young men would be "warned out" of town instead of being invited to stay and acquire a farm. There is no record of anyone in the Colony having owned a Negro slave, although every other New England colony had a few, and Rhode Island became active in the slave trade.

It may seem strange that in this land of plain living and hard work there should be any poor people. But it was as true of Plymouth as of Palestine: ". . . ye have the poor always with you." Children were left orphans, houses burned down, some men were shiftless and some women were slatterns, and many a family faced winter without food or fuel or even shelter. So, as Jesus taught Christians to feed the hungry and clothe the naked, the Plymouth people did their best.

Taking care of the poor was a job for the town, not the Colony. In Plymouth, for instance, when the first board of selectmen was elected in 1649, they were given power to inquire into "the state and condition of the poor," to see "that the poor be comfortably provided for," and that their provisions "be not unnecessarily embezzled, misspent and made away in the summer season before the winter and time of hard things come." And if the selectmen found any aged or crippled poor who could not work, they were empowered to raise taxes for their relief.

Plymouth Town was fortunate in having a special donation for this purpose. James Sherley, one of the London Adventurers who helped to finance the *May-*

flower, sent out a heifer in 1624 for the use of the poor. This heifer, bred to the town bull, throve to such good purpose that by 1638 she had twelve descendants, which were lent to poor people who couldn't afford to buy a cow; and other calves of hers were sold to add to the poor fund. Bradford, Prence, Willet, and other leading men were a committee of the town to handle "the poor's stock"; and, for a quarter-century after her arrival, Sherley's heifer's offspring were being distributed annually.

In those small communities, private and neighborly charity took care of most cases of misfortune, but the towns often made contributions of food and fuel to the needy. Children left orphans were added to some other family, in the same status as servants. This system was far more humane than the later one of herding the poor into orphan asylums and "poor farms."

Readers may regard the life we have described as a very drab one for young people. They had no modern forms of amusement or methods of transportation, and were forbidden to "date" without father's or master's permission. Actually it was a very full and interesting life, because there was something for every child to do from the time he could walk; he had his place in the family team. For amusement, he whittled toys out of wood, made dolls out of rags, and played a game called stool-ball with a leather ball stuffed with feathers. In winter, he coasted on a homemade sled, skated on homemade skates, walked over deep snow on "rackets" (snowshoes) that the Indians taught him to make and use; or fished for pickerel through the ice on the big ponds. In summer, he went fishing and swimming when father could spare him from the corn-fields—but never on Sunday! Best of all, from the modern point of view, he had a minimum of book learning. His education was finished as soon as he could do a little simple arithmetic, write his name, and read the Bible; and there was not much but the Bible to read. He learned by doing, from his elders; and he learned self-control by having to handle and tame a variety of animals, and to row and sail a boat. His father taught him to fear God and honor the King and the Governor; he took pride in being an English subject, and looked forward to becoming a Freeman of the oldest colony in New England. And, strict though the Puritan religion was, it taught him that he was a child of God, and that God had brought him into the world for a definite purpose; that if he believed in God and obeyed His commandments so far as human nature would permit, he would enjoy eternal life.

There is no need to pity the Pilgrim boys and girls. They really enjoyed the life that they led, and they envied nobody.

4. Farming, Trade, and Business

The prices that Plymouth obtained for cattle and hogs in the 1630's are astonishing, in comparison with the value of other things. William Wright's house and garden, for instance, were valued only at ten pounds, and seldom was any house valued at more than twice that; but his "1 cow and 1 steer calf" were worth twenty pounds. Francis

Eaton, a Plymouth carpenter, left a cow worth twenty pounds and a "cow calfe" worth twelve pounds; but his best suit of clothes was valued at only one pound and his chest of carpenter's tools added up to only a little more.[9] And a day's wages was only a shilling or eighteenpence. If Mr. Sherley's heifer hadn't done so well, the poor would have been unable to own a cow.

Yet even when the price fell, their cattle were the most valuable possessions of the Plymouth colonists. A cow was a part of the family. As proof of it, although dogs and horses are never mentioned by name in Plymouth Colony wills, the names of the cattle often are. It may amuse you to know some of these names:

Of oxen, always in pairs: Buck and Duke, Spark and Swad, Quick and Benbo, Duke and Butler.

Of cows and heifers: Motley, Symkins, Damson, Prosper, Thrivewell, Cherry, Colley, Brown, Gentle, Moose, Blacking, Nubbin, Pretty, Daisy, Bunny, and Traveler. Perhaps Traveler came over from England; but I suspect that she was a leaper of fences.

Cattle were as important to a Plymouth family as a donkey to a Sicilian or Greek peasant. They furnished milk, veal, beef, and hides for clothing and shoes. All plowing, pulling up stumps, and transport by two-wheeled cart was done by ox-power.

Horse raising became as important as cattle raising, if not more so, because a market for work and saddle horses had opened in the West Indies and the Southern

---

[9] We remind the reader here that one pound (£1) was roughly five dollars; one shilling (1s.) twenty-five cents.

colonies. Horses were kept in barns during the winter and the mares bred so that they would foal in the spring. Mares, foals, and all horses not being used by the family were then turned out to pasture in the common lands of each township. Every town had to have a distinctive brand for its horses, and every owner a distinctive mark, usually some sort of slit in one ear. Fences now had to be made "horse-high" as well as "ox-strong" and "hog-tight," so that the horses would not desert the woody pastures for luscious fields of green corn, or meadows where the hay had to be saved for winter fodder.

In the early fall there was a round-up, great fun for the young men and boys. All the horses they could catch were collected in the town pound, or some other enclosure, and sorted out according to brand and mark. Each owner then decided which ones he wished to sell, and one or more young men undertook to drive the town's collection to Boston. Plymouth Town became so much annoyed by herds of Boston-bound horses from the Cape being driven along Main Street and lunching off the flower and vegetable gardens that the constables were ordered to take special measures for protection of property.

The Colony itself made the rules about branding and marking, and regulated horse raising. Unmarked stray horses that were picked up had to be "cryed" (advertised) at two sessions of a court; and if not claimed within a year, could be kept by the finder. Horses running in from the Bay Colony or Rhode Island, "causing damage and annoyance to English and Indians alike," were to be treated as strays; the "foreign" owner could get them back only if he paid damages. And, in order to keep up the breed of Old Colony horses and eliminate runts, no stallions under thirteen hands high and over two years old were permitted to run free during the summer.

Naturally the young men took to racing their horses along the highways, and this became such a traffic menace that it had to be forbidden. But it was very fortunate that New England had plenty of horses when King Philip's War broke out, and that every young man knew how to ride; for by mounting the troops they were able to catch up with fast-moving Indians.

Farming was so taken for granted as the main business of everyone in the Old Colony that we have very little information about it. We do know, however, that the principal crop through the length and breadth of the Colony was Indian corn. And we are fortunate to have a detailed account, from the pen of Governor Winthrop of Connecticut, as to how it was cultivated in 1660.

The corn of that period was just as it had come from the Indians; rather small, nubbly ears, the kernels colored not only yellow but red, blue, green, and black. The ground was prepared by plows and harrows, or even with hoes alone, Indian fashion. Corn hills were laid out six feet apart. In each hill four or five kernels were planted, together with two or three fish to "nourish" the corn, as the Governor put it. If alewives were not available, any fish offal would do.

After the green blades appeared, furrows were dug crisscross by a plow or hoe, and the earth hilled up so that the cornfield presented a checkerboard appearance with a hill in the middle of each square. Beans were often planted in the same hill as the corn, using the cornstalks as poles. In the intersections of the furrows, squashes and pumpkins were planted; and their vines, spreading all around, served to keep the weeds down. Some farmers, however, did not believe in this, and used the spaces between the hills to plant turnips or parsnips.

Corn was used in a variety of ways for man and beast. It was eaten green as "roasting ears"; parched so that the kernel was partly cooked and became easily digested; pounded in a mortar or ground in a grist mill to make bread, hasty pudding, and Indian pudding; treated with lye to make samp or hominy. Beer was often made out of it, for lack of wheat malt. The stalks were left on the ground as winter fodder for cattle, and the grain was also used to fatten cattle and swine. Corn was the greatest gift from the red man to the white.

Many kinds of apples, pears, plums, and quinces were planted in the orchards of the Old Colony, apples predominating. As most of the varieties that they had were soft summer apples, and as the colonists always shook them off the trees, they did not keep well and had to be cut up and sun-dried for winter use. But a large proportion of the apples went into cider, the favorite drink of the Old Colony farmer.

Owing to the habit of cows and other animals of breaking into cornfields or orchards and raising havoc, the Colony and the towns were always fussing about fences. The common fence in most parts of the Colony was a loose stone wall; but on Cape Cod and in other regions, where stone was scarce, fences of split chestnut or round cedar were built. All had to be "ox-strong" and "hog-tight." Pigs were so clever at worming through a fence and rooting up crops that they had to be yoked and ringed, except in winter.[1]

The keeping up of fences was very important. Robert Frost's poem "Mending Wall" tells of a custom that started very early in the Old Colony: neighbors walking along a stone wall in early spring, to pick up and replace the stones that winter frost or animals had thrown down. Then, as now, "good fences make good neighbors."

The wave of prosperity based on cattle raising came to an abrupt halt in 1641, because civil war had broken out in England and Puritans had stopped emigrating. Corn now "would buy nothing," wrote Governor Winthrop. The price of a cow fell off to four or five pounds. Many a good bossy was now slaughtered and eaten because there was no market for her. As a Boston poet put it, in an early almanac:

> *That since the mighty Cow her crown hath lost*
> *In every place she's made to rule the roast.*

And, Winthrop adds, the depression caused the New England people to concentrate on "making" fish and cutting lumber products for export to the West Indies.

This "fall of cow," as it was called in New England— and we may fairly call it the earliest crash in the stock market—affected Plymouth even more than the Bay Col-

---

[1] The hog yoke was a sort of wooden frame in the form of the letter A, which was fastened around the pig's neck. The ring, inserted in piggy's nose, prevented him from rooting.

ony. For Plymouth had gone in heavily for raising cattle and corn for the Boston market, and by this time the fur trade had declined. The Old Colony tried the same remedy as the Bay. Already she had some experience in building small vessels; a pinnace with a ketch rig, about forty feet long, was built at Duxbury in 1640 for forty pounds. Next year, the leading men of Plymouth chipped in £200 or more to build a "barque" of forty to fifty tons for the West Indies trade. But what became of her we do not know.

Trade with the West Indies was the economic salvation of New England. Planters in the English, French, and Dutch islands from Barbados to St. Croix preferred to employ their labor growing tobacco or sugar cane, and to import all luxuries and many necessities. New England found the islands a wonderful market for corn, salt fish, pickled beef and pork, oak pipe staves to make hogsheads, and shooks to make boxes, lumber to build houses. Even horses were exported to provide power for the (literally) one-horse sugar mills of that era, and also live cattle and poultry.

Plymouth Colony ports seldom entered this trade directly; they were feeders to Boston, Salem, Newport, or New London. Sloops and shallops carried local products to one of those larger ports, where they were transhipped, and brought back West India goods, and clothing, tools, and luxuries which the merchants had imported from England. The great demand for fish in the West Indies made it worth while for the towns from Scituate to Eastham to "make fish" for the foreign market. And many Plymouth boys "shipped foreign" in Boston vessels.

The West Indies in the seventeenth century were very much wealthier than the mainland colonies, and a winter spent in a voyage down there was lots of fun, and profitable, too. Big boys came back home with pockets full of Spanish dollars ("pieces of eight") and boasting that they had seen "mountains of sugar, rivers of rum, and fish that fly in the air." One Pilgrim mother said she could believe the first two, but flying fish she could not swallow, and scolded her sailor son for telling such a whopping lie!

How did the New Englanders, who had no previous experience in seafaring, find their way to the West Indies? It was not too difficult. As one old sea captain put it: "Sail south till your butter melts, then west!" The little ketches and barks, making a wide sweep outside Cape Cod, Nantucket Shoals, and Bermuda, sailed south until the skipper saw by the altitude of the North Star that he was about on the latitude of Barbados, and then turned west. The time to start was in the late fall, when the hurricane season was over and you could count on the tradewinds to take you easily from island to island.

This trade had grown to such an extent in 1662 that the Old Colony laid export taxes on boards and planks, barrel staves and headings, tar, iron bars—and oysters! The last item is surprising; apparently the West India planters were demanding Wellfleet pickled oysters.

Little actual money reached Plymouth Colony; most of the imported silver dollars were spent in Boston, and many a boy grew to manhood without seeing any bigger coin than a Massachusetts pine-tree shilling. It was a barter economy. Everyone kept accounts in pounds, shillings, and pence but little money changed hands; and there was nothing in the entire Colony like a modern shop or store. But that did not seem strange, because in England at that time there were no shops except in London and the shire towns. Plymouth Colony followed the English practice of doing most of its trading at markets or fairs. Plymouth Town had a market every Thursday, and a May fair; Duxbury had an October fair; almost every other settlement had a market day, and the larger ones held annual fairs. On market days everyone who had something to sell or who wanted to buy, and many who just wanted to talk, came to the village green or town square. A fisherman with an extra barrel or two of pickled mackerel might sell some of it to a farmer in exchange for salt beef or a live hog. Chickens, eggs, butter, and all manner of farm produce were traded; much of it to a local merchant who sold it in Boston.

The annual fair brought lots of people by boat or trail from the other towns; it was the time for visiting friends and relatives as well as for trading. Indians brought great heaps of baskets, brooms, and wooden ware; peddlers in sloops from Boston or Newport spread out a tempting array of knives and cutlery, pins and needles, combs and brushes, and all manner of small wares, and were ready to take country produce in exchange, or salt fish, tar, and barrel staves. Fur traders from the Kennebec and local trappers had attractive parcels of beaver, otter, and musquash for sale—even a few mink, then esteemed only a little better than tabby cat. Flocks of sheep, herds of cattle, coops of poultry, and even a few horses were driven in for sale, and the usually quiet green or square resounded with moos, baas, neighs, barks, clucks, and the hissing of indignant geese.

The constable strode about with his brass-tipped black rod of office, to see that the Indians got no liquor and that nobody got drunk; but, all the same, everyone had a gay time chaffering, swapping, and gossiping. The young men showed off the paces of colts they had raised, and bought ribbons for their girls; young matrons exchanged cow "Daisy" or heifer "Bunny" for a dress straight from London; men talked crops and discussed the likelihood of war with France or Spain or the Dutch, and wondered what effect it would have on the price of corn and beef.

The nearest thing to a permanent store in the Colony was the warehouse of a merchant who collected the products of farm, fishery, and forest for export, and brought in molasses, wines and liquors, clothing, hardware, and various English and West Indies goods. Rum came in about 1670, and was at first frowned upon as a disreputable sailor's drink.

The most modern business established in Plymouth Colony was the iron industry. Throughout eastern New England there was a fair amount of iron ore in swamps and on the bottom of ponds; the problem was how to smelt it. Around 1643, two groups of English capitalists set up iron works at Saugus and at Braintree in the Bay Colony. With imported Scots labor—prisoners taken by Cromwell in the English Civil War—they set up a furnace or "bloomery" where the ore was melted by roaring fires of oak wood, flowing out red-hot into sand molds where it cooled off and became iron "pigs." The pig iron was beaten by a trip hammer run by water power until impurities were expelled, and it became wrought or bar iron; and this iron was fashioned into nails, spikes, kettles, skillets, anchors, chains, and other useful articles. The old iron works at Saugus, lately restored, are the best example anywhere of an American colonial factory.

The seat of this industry in Plymouth Colony was at Taunton, at the head of navigation on the Taunton River, which flows into Narragansett Bay. That settlement was founded by English emigrants in 1630 who purchased land from Massasoit at two shillings an acre. In 1637 the population was increased by the arrival of forty-eight-year-old Elizabeth Pole, described by Governor Winthrop as "a gentlewoman, an ancient maid" of Taunton in Old England. She walked through the woods from Boston, driving her cattle and accompanied by her brother William and sundry servants. After purchasing another tract of land from the Indians, she persuaded the people to name the place Taunton, and Taunton was shortly after given representation to the General Court. Members of the Cobb, Morton, Deane, and Macy families were already there, or came shortly after. Iron ore was discovered on the banks of Two-Mile River; a stock company with capital of £600 was organized, Elizabeth Pole being a prominent stockholder. The Leonard brothers and Ralph Russell, former officers of the Braintree iron works, were invited to come, and in 1656 the Taunton Iron Works opened. They were so successful that iron bars became currency in Taunton; taxes and the schoolteacher's salary were paid in this "iron money," and the town became the most prosperous in the Colony. A visitor, in 1660, described it as "a pleasant place, seated among the windings and turnings of a handsome river, and hath good conveyance to Boston by cart." The Taunton Iron Works were operated until 1876.

Apart from these iron works there was nothing you could call an organized industry in Plymouth Colony. Almost every town had a few simple specialists such as carpenters, boat builders, bricklayers, blacksmiths, millers, brewers, and cobblers. Every town had a minister and some had a physician; but even these professional gentlemen owned farms and grew most of the food for their families. There were no such extremes of wealth as in Virginia, New York, or Massachusetts Bay; everyone worked at something, and almost everyone made a fair living.

Altogether it was a simple society with a primitive economy and a static social system. There was no printing press or silversmith as in Boston, there were few schools and little evidence of intellectual life. Apart from the poems of John Saffin that we have quoted, Governor Bradford's noble History, and Nathaniel Morton's *New England's Memoriall* (which is largely a poor paraphrase of Bradford), Plymouth Colony produced no literature. In this, as in foreign trade, the Colony was a backwater, sheltered from the main currents of New England life.

But whenever there was trouble with the Indians, Plymouth men were up in front, shooting!

CHAPTER IV The Wisdom of

Benjamin Franklin

Many great men in history have had little or no sense of humor, and George Washington was one of them; but Benjamin Franklin, the most versatile genius in American history, not only had a sense of humor but was one of the few people who could get a laugh out of George. The story he liked best was Ben's reply to the stuffy Englishman in 1775 who protested that it was foul ball for the Yankee minutemen to fire at British redcoats from behind stone walls. "Why?" said Ben. "Didn't those walls have two sides?" George relished this so well that when he visited Lexington, fourteen years later, he told it to his guides, astonishing them with roars of laughter. And like most of Franklin's jokes, this had a moral to it—don't be mad at your enemy if he is smarter than you, but try to be smarter yourself.

Franklin's humor, as revealed in his *Poor Richard's Almanack*, is always kindly, often earthy to the point of coarseness, but never bitter. He makes fun of pretense and stuffiness, but never sneers at poverty or ignorance.

He is whimsical, as in his "Drinker's Dictionary," where he gives more than 100 terms for drunkenness—some of which, like "fuddled," "stew'd," and "half seas over," have endured; but most, like "cherry merry," "as dizzy as a goose," and "loose in the hilts," have gone down the drain. He was a master of political satire, as in that fake edict of a German king proposing to tax England because the Anglo-Saxons originally came from Germany, and he excelled in the typically American humor of exaggeration. For instance, he warns passengers sailing down Delaware Bay in August not to be alarmed at hearing "a confus'd rattling noise, like a shower of hail on a cake of ice." It is the season of fevers and agues in the "lower counties"—the present state of Delaware—and the noise is the chattering of the inhabitants' teeth!

Born in Boston in 1706, missing the Puritan century by only six years, Ben Franklin was three years older than Dr. Samuel Johnson and ten years older than Thomas Gray. Every other leader of the American Revolution belonged to a generation later than his; Washington was twenty-six years younger; Jefferson, thirty-seven years younger; Hamilton might have been Ben's grandson and was, in fact, only five years older than his grandson William Temple Franklin. Benjamin Franklin was old enough to have called on the Rev. Cotton Mather, who when approaching a low-hanging beam in his parsonage, between the living room and the library, gave young Ben a piece of advice he always remembered and acted upon: "You are young and have the world before you; stoop as you go through it, and you will miss many hard bumps."

Expediency, or, accept the second best if you cannot get the best, might have been Franklin's motto. He was always advising it in his almanacs, as: "Write with the learned, pronounce with the vulgar," and "Keep your eyes wide open before marriage, half shut afterwards."

Ben Franklin set the pattern of the American success story. Withdrawn from Boston Latin School within a year because, as tenth son and fifteenth child in a tallow chandler's family, his father could not afford the small tuition fee, he became, by his own efforts, one of the most learned men of his age. He would have enjoyed enduring fame as a scientist and philosopher had he never dabbled in politics. "Doctor Franklin" he was called, because of honorary degrees from Harvard, Yale, St. Andrews, and Oxford; he could put "F.R.S." after his name as a fellow of the Royal Society of London and was elected corresponding member of most of the learned societies of Europe. At home he was the only American leader except Washington who commanded respect and confidence throughout the Thirteen Colonies, four of which, New Jersey, Massachusetts, Pennsylvania, and Georgia, appointed him their agent, or official lobbyist, in England. And his popularity went deep; he had the confidence of all classes. Robert Morris, Philip Livingston, and Cadwallader Colden were proud to have him to dinner; yet the frontiersmen of North Carolina proposed that he "represent the unhappy state of this Province to His Majesty."

Ben was as American as clam chowder and johnnycake, but equally at home in England, where he spent almost twenty years prior to 1776, and in France, where he had popular renown and great influence. A pioneer in experimental physics, especially in the new branch of electricity, he was in touch with everything else that went on in the scientific world; yet he could also make practical inventions such as the lightning rod and the Franklin stove. (Incidentally, the so-called Franklin stoves now found in antique shops are much less effective than the original "Pennsylvanian Fire-Places" which Franklin invented in 1740. This metal fireplace included an air box over which the hot combustion gases passed on their way to the chimney. Outside air was drawn in through a duct, circulated through the air box around baffles, and passed out into the room.)

When he crossed the Atlantic he studied winds and currents to such good purpose that he could instruct Yankee skippers how to work the Gulf Stream to best advantage. A conservative until the very eve of the Revolution and an advocate of compromise with Britain, Franklin became in 1775 one of the strongest exponents of American independence; and, although seventy years old when American independence was declared, he was one of the more radical Revolutionary leaders.

Franklin never made much money, but was generous with what he had, and a public benefactor. He refused to have his inventions patented; everyone could profit from them. One of his legacies, operated under sagacious principles that he laid down, still provides the Franklin Medals for top scholars in the Boston schools; another still contributes income to the Franklin Institute of Philadelphia. His many private charities were unobtrusive; most touching were his efforts to preserve the self-respect of his sister, Jane Mecom, by setting her up in business with the old family recipe for crown soap. And he was a most accomplished man. He could fix anything around the house and tell others how to do it in his annual almanac. He could play the violin, guitar, and harp, and he invented a new musical instrument which he called the armonica, on the principle of the musical glasses. Mozart and Beethoven composed music for the armonica, and Queen Marie Antoinette, among others, learned to play it.

A great man by any standard, Franklin was a universal genius, great in a variety of ways—as printer, philanthropist, statesman, man of science; as naturalist and humanist, and writer whose *Autobiography* and *Poor Richard's Almanack* had an international vogue. Nor was Franklin content to write literature; he organized it, as he did everything else. He organized the Philadelphia Library, the first important semi-public library in the Colonies; the College of Philadelphia, which became the University of Pennsylvania; and a "Junto" or discussion club, which eventually became the American Philosophical Society, our senior learned society.

Franklin's secret, the thing that "made him tick" and pulled every aspect of his mind together, was his love of people. Not people in the abstract, like Karl Marx, Henry George, and other dreary prophets of progress, but people in particular, and of all kinds. He liked intellectuals, businessmen, workingmen, children, and Negroes; not only Americans but also Englishmen, Frenchmen, and

Europeans of a dozen other nations. Not that he had any illusions about people. He knew them at their worst as well as their best, but he accepted them. Note this remarkable prophecy written in 1780:

The rapid progress *true* science now makes, occasions my regretting sometimes that I was born so soon. It is impossible to imagine the height to which may be carried, in a thousand years, the power of man over matter. We may perhaps learn to deprive large masses of their gravity, and give them absolute levity. . . . Agriculture may diminish its labor and double its produce; all diseases may by sure means be prevented or cured . . . O that *moral science* were in as fair a way of improvement, that men would cease to be *wolves* to one another and that human beings would at length learn what they now improperly call humanity!

He talked with English and French statesmen as an equal; yet he was as homely and comfortable as an old shoe. If you had been a young man in 1776 calling on the great ones of the day, you would have been overawed by George Washington, and Sam Adams you would have found rather grim; Alexander Hamilton would have made you feel very small and stupid, Patrick Henry would have made you a speech, and John Adams would have talked your head off. But old Ben would have made you at home. He would have asked after your parents, and probably would have known them, or at least about them; he would then have asked you about yourself, drawn you out, and sent you away with some good advice, a warm handclasp, and a smile you would have remembered all your life. The same would be true if the visitor were a young girl, especially a pretty girl. "Caty" Ray, a lively lass of twenty-three who happened to meet Franklin at his brother's house in Boston when he was forty-eight, became his friend for life. For more than thirty years they maintained an intimate correspondence, charming on both sides though rather illiterate on hers; and Ben's last letter, written shortly before his death, ended: "Among the felicities of my life I reckon your friendship, which I shall remember with pleasure as long as that life lasts."

It was because he loved people so much, that he hated war profoundly. After peace had been concluded in 1783, largely owing to his efforts, he wrote: "At length we are in peace, God be praised, and long, very long, may it continue. All wars are follies, very expensive, and very mischievous ones. When will mankind be convinced of this, and agree to settle their differences by arbitration?" Yet Franklin hated cruelty and injustice even more than he hated war. Outrages on humanity, such as those perpetrated by the Pennsylvania frontiersmen on the Moravian Indians, evoked savage indignation from his usually serene and tolerant mind. His last public paper, in 1790, was written in favor of the abolition of Negro slavery; and for it he was bitterly attacked in the United States Senate. No doctrinaire pacifist, he supported the three principal wars of his time. He used the wisdom of the serpent to get around the pacifism of Pennsylvania Quakers and persuade them to co-operate in the French and Indian War.

Hopeless of abolishing war in his day, Franklin made every effort, through treaties and international agreements, to render war less horrible by safeguarding the rights of neutrals and of noncombatants; by obtaining agreements that farmers, fishermen, and other civilians would not be molested by armies and fleets. He hoped to confine war to professional forces and to make it less frequent by recourse to arbitration. The United States followed this policy until the present century; but between the Hague Convention of 1907 and the London Naval Conference of 1909 there came a turning point, and we joined other nations on the road to total war and, possibly, total destruction.

Franklin's life passed through many phases—the poor boy of a large family, the Boston journeyman printer, the young man making his way in Philadelphia. Following one of his favorite quotations from the Bible, "It is better to marry than to burn," Ben married his landlady's daughter Deborah. "Debby," almost illiterate, already married to a sailor who had simply disappeared, shared few of Franklin's interests and prevented his being accepted by the polite society of his adopted city. "How the scum rises!" remarked a Philadelphia matron when Franklin's grandson moved uptown. But that sort of thing didn't bother Ben. He was no status seeker; he accepted every social contact that came his way, and in all his vast correspondence that has been preserved there is not one complaint of being slighted or snubbed. No man ever born had less class-consciousness. He never attempted to conceal his working-class origin; in his last will and testament he described himself as "Benjamin Franklin, printer." He was not ashamed of his poor relations, who were both numerous and importunate. Many people, when he rose to fame, became his enemies and did their best to pull him down; but he never retaliated, and in his thousands of letters I have found no unkind word about anyone.

Poor Richard's Almanack, from 1733 on, is full of epigrams and mottoes that we still use in common speech, often forgetting whence they came, such as:

Time is money.
Snug as a bug in a rug.
Keep one's nose to the grindstone.
Necessity never made a good bargain.
Three may keep a secret if two of them are dead.
Experience keeps a dear school, but fools will learn in no other.

And these, now forgotten, deserve a revival:

Fish and visitors smell in three days.
There are no fools so troublesome as those that have wit.
There are three faithful friends, an old wife, an old dog, and ready money.
None but the well-bred man knows how to confess a fault, or acknowledge himself in error.

Ten or twelve years after the almanac started, Franklin began his electrical and scientific work. In 1748 he retired from active printing and bookselling, which gave him leisure for writing and science. His *Experiments and Observations on Electricity*, printed at London in 1751, was translated into French, Italian, and German. The book earned its author several honorary degrees, and the Copley Medal of the Royal Society of London, and made him a leading figure in the world of science. These experiments, of which the famous one with kite and key was the best known but not the most important, were a notable contribution to knowledge. Franklin was responsible for the concept of positive and negative electricity; he made the first electric battery and armature; he explained how the Leyden jar, the first electrical condenser, worked. He would have liked to devote his entire life to science, but was too public-spirited to confine himself to that. He served as deputy postmaster-general for the English Colonies for twenty-one years, and very efficiently. He entered Pennsylvania politics early, and became a member of the Assembly. He organized logistic support for British armies in the interior during the Old French and Indian War, and he represented Pennsylvania at the Albany Congress of 1754. Three years later the Assembly sent him to England to try to persuade the Penn family to allow their millions of acres of wild land to pay a small tax to the province.

In England, Franklin remained for seventeen years, most of the time as agent for the assemblies of several colonies. He made a host of friends among scientists, men of letters, economists, and politicians; he promoted the scheme for a new Vandalia colony on the Ohio; he met Doctor Johnson as member of a charitable society, the Associates of Doctor Bray, which set up schools for Negro children in colonial towns. He frequently contributed to the London newspapers articles, letters, and squibs supporting the rights of the colonists, the most humorous called "Rules by which a Great Empire may be Reduced to a Small One," which he dedicated to one of the leading British ministers. At the same time he wrote to his American friends begging them to moderate their demands and respect law and order, since time was working for them.

This policy got him in wrong with the colonial radicals. He spoke different languages to his English and his American friends, precisely because he was trying to moderate the extreme demands of each side and to find a formula by which American liberty could be preserved within the British Empire. That, of course, exposed him to the charge of hypocrisy. His position as colonial agent became very shaky in 1773. Sam Adams attacked him, partly because of his moderation, but mostly because he regarded Franklin as a wicked old man. Debby refused to cross the ocean, and so never came to London with Ben, who was reported to be leading the life of young Boswell; and in his writings he took an earthy, practical view of sex that outraged Puritanical sentiment. Curiously enough, it was Franklin's realistic attitude toward sex that inspired the vicious attack on his reputation, in *Studies in Classic American Literature* (1923), by D. H. Lawrence, who, though far from a Puritan in sexual matters, seems to have expected everyone else to be one.

Franklin worked hard to prevent a breach with the mother country, but when it became clear that Parliament would not repeal the Coercive Acts, he realized that his mission had failed. In March 1775 he sailed from England for the last time as a subject of King George. The very day after his arrival in Philadelphia he was chosen by the Pennsylvania Assembly a delegate to the Continental Congress.

In Congress or out, Franklin was no great or original political thinker. In politics he was an opportunist, or pragmatist, to give opportunism its modern philosophical term. His one test of a constitution, or of a political arrangement, was: "Will it work?" The British Empire before 1763 worked very well, so he wished to continue it, or restore it as it had been, rather than break off. Similar was his attitude toward religion. As a young man he had been a typical eighteenth-century deist, but he abandoned deism because "this doctrine might be true, but was not very useful." He observed that public morality was essential to good government and that organized Christianity was the best promoter of public morality; so he supported churches and even occasionally attended them.

Franklin placed a high value on conciliation and compromise in politics. He did not like the result of the Federal Convention of 1787, of which he was the oldest and most experienced member, because he disliked checks and balances, and wanted no United States Senate. Yet such was his common sense and his respect for the opinions of others that he accepted and supported the Federal Constitution instead of standing out against it as did George Mason, Elbridge Gerry, and other members whose vanity had been wounded because their pet ideas had not been adopted. The famous speech he delivered near the end of the convention expresses his attitude perfectly:

I confess that there are several parts of this Constitution which I do not at present approve, but I am not sure I shall never approve them; for having lived long, I have experienced many instances of being obliged, by better information or fuller consideration, to change opinions . . . which I once thought right, but found to be otherwise. . . .
Thus I consent, sir, to this Constitution because I expect no better, and because I am not sure that it is not the best. The

opinions I have had of its errors I sacrifice to the public good; I have never whispered a syllable of them abroad; within these walls they were born, and here they shall die. If every one of us in returning to our constituents were to report the objections he has had to it, and endeavor to gain partisans in support of them, we might prevent its being generally received. . . .

Franklin may therefore be considered one of the founding fathers of American democracy, since no democratic government can last long without conciliation and compromise. And the mere knowledge that he was in favor of the Constitution did more to win acceptance from the common people of America than all the learned, close-reasoned articles in *The Federalist*, admirable as they are.

In diplomacy, too, Franklin was a genius. The sending of him to France to represent the Continental Congress was a master stroke; for in France he already had a great reputation as a man of science, and as "Bonhomme Richard." The French government, of course, favored him because he represented American resistance to their hereditary enemy; and all who were dreaming of liberty for France revered him as a signer of the Declaration of Independence. His book on electrical experiments, which had been translated, paraphrased, and published more than once, gave him high prestige among scientists and philosophers. An edition of *Oeuvres de M. Franclin* had appeared in 1773; and an enterprising Paris bookseller had translated his *The Way to Wealth* and a selection of his proverbs and witty sayings in the almanacs as *La Science de Bonhomme Richard*. This turned out to be even more important than his work on electricity in enhancing Franklin's reputation.

The simple yet witty moral teachings in these maxims made a tremendous appeal. Edition followed edition off the French press; it was even referred to as the "Bible of the Eighteenth Century," and a royal official advised the use of it in connection with the catechism. *Bonhomme Richard* proved that a scientist could be religious and creative, not merely a destructive critic of religion and a puller-down of ancient institutions, as most of the French men of science had been. The maxims were acceptable to the Church, and made Franklin a favorite figure among the people at large. The ancient warfare between science and religion seemed to be ended. It was Franklin, more than any other person, who convinced the average Catholic bourgeois that natural science was not to be feared as impious and anti-Christian, but a good thing which would react in a beneficial way on human life.

Hitherto, little effort had been made to define the limits between science and religion. It was generally supposed to be immoral to assert a scientific cause for phenomena such as earthquakes, shooting stars, thunder, and lightning. Thus Franklin's proof of electricity's causing lightning became very significant. It had an impact comparable to that in our time of Einstein's theory of relativity. It took out of the field of religion something earlier classified as an act of God and included it in natural science. Yet nobody could deny that Franklin was a religious man, that he believed in God and called himself a Christian.

Franklin behaved in France with great sagacity. He did not mix with the people or drive through the streets waving his hat and soliciting cheers; he lived aloof in the Hôtel Valentinois at Passy and seldom appeared in public. The rumor that he was a Quaker seemed to be confirmed because he allowed himself to be presented to the King without a wig or elaborate court dress. That was just an accident—the wig did not come in time—but it was all to the good because Quakers were the only Christian sect favored by the philosophers. Franklin also used his membership in the Masonic fraternity to good effect; the Masonic Lodge of the Nine Sisters, which he joined in Paris and of which he became Grand Master, helped to mobilize public opinion in favor of French intervention in the War of Independence.

One of the warmest tributes to Franklin's influence and standing in France came from the pen of John Paul Jones, whose naval efforts he consistently supported, despite countless difficulties. Jones wrote to Robert Morris: "I know the great and good in this kingdom better, perhaps, than any other American who has appeared in Europe since the treaty of alliance, and if my testimony could add anything to Franklin's reputation I would witness the universal veneration and esteem with which his name inspires all ranks, not only at Versailles and all over this kingdom, but also in Spain and Holland. And I can add from the testimony of the first characters of other nations that with them envy is dumb when the name of Franklin is but mentioned."

John Adams, Franklin's colleague at Paris, has left an amusing account of the doctor's working day as a diplomat. Hard-working, conscientious John tried to get the doctor to do business, or at least to sign papers, before breakfast, but seldom with success. He breakfasted late; and as soon as it was over, carriages began arriving at the Hôtel Valentinois with all sorts of people, "some philosophers, academicians and economists," some literary men; "but by far the greater part were women and children, come to have the pleasure of telling stories among their acquaintances about his simplicity, his bald head and scattering straight hairs." These visitors occupied all his time until the hour to dress for dinner, between one and two o'clock. He was invited to dine out almost every day and seldom declined. After dinner he sometimes attended the play, sometimes a session of the academy or a lodge meeting, but more often to visit one of his lady friends and take tea.

"Some of these ladies," says Adams, "I knew, as Madame Helvétius, Madame Brillon, Madame Chaumont, Madame Le Ray, and others whom I never knew and never enquired for. After tea the evening was spent in hearing the ladies sing and play upon their pianofortes and other instrument of musick, and in various games as cards, chess, backgammon." Franklin, however, never played anything but chess or checkers. "In these agreeable and important occupations and amusements," says Adams, "the afternoon and evening was spent, and he came home at all hours from nine to twelve o'clock at night. This course of life contributed to his pleasure and I believe to his health and longevity."

To one of these ladies, Madame Helvétius, wealthy widow of a noted philosopher, Franklin proposed marriage when he was more than seventy and she was but a few years younger. The young, beautiful, and amiable

Madame Brillon de Jouy was willing to sit on Franklin's lap and to let him play chess with her when she was soaking in one of those enormous covered bathtubs of the period, but no other favors beyond that would she allow. Madame Le Ray de Chaumont—she was one person and not two, as John Adams seemed to remember—was the wife of the owner of the Hôtel Valentinois, in a wing of which Franklin lived. Her husband was a practical shipowner who handled much of the unneutral aid given by France to America before the treaty was signed in 1778. She became the first of a succession of French mistresses to John Paul Jones, when that gallant captain arrived in France as commanding officer of U.S.S. *Ranger*.

For all that John Adams said, Franklin managed to write a surprising number of letters, by dictating them to his secretaries at breakfast or between social engagements. And he did the main work of the American mission, through personal contacts. Far more effective than formal notes were a whispered conversation at the play, a hint to a cabinet minister's mistress, a confidential chat at the Masonic Lodge.

Franklin was also keenly interested in aeronautics. He was a friend of the Montgolfier brothers, who made the first balloon ascensions. "We think of nothing here at present but of flying," he wrote from Paris in 1783. "The balloons engross all attention." John Jeffries, who made the first balloon crossing of the English Channel, brought Franklin from London the world's first airmail letter.

Scientists and intellectuals of many countries were eager to meet Franklin. The Rev. Samuel Domien, a globetrotting Orthodox priest from Rumania, sought out the sage at Philadelphia and exchanged notes on electricity and the natural laziness of mankind. The Abbé Boscovich of Ragusa (Dubrovnik), author of a leading work on natural philosophy with which Franklin was familiar, called on him at Passy and suggested that they draft a commercial treaty between the republics of America and Ragusa.

Thus Benjamin Franklin was a universal genius, more so than any other man of his day, American or European; one from whose writings the student of almost any subject, from orchids to oceanography, or from politics to population growth, can learn something. He was the embodiment of what we like to call the American spirit—idealistic but practical, principled but expedient, optimistic for human betterment and the world's future.

One of his last letters, of March 9, 1790, was written in answer to President Ezra Stiles of Yale. "You desire to know something of my religion," he says. "It is the first time I have been questioned upon it." (Who but a president of Yale would have dared?) "But I cannot take your curiosity amiss, and shall endeavour in a few words to gratify it." He affirms his belief in God as the Creator of the Universe, and in immortality. He expresses some doubt of the divinity of Jesus; but with characteristic humor adds that he will not dogmatize on the subject, "having never studied it, and think it needless to busy myself with it now, when I expect soon an opportunity to know the truth with less trouble."

He had less than six weeks to wait.

As "Poor Richard" he had remarked in one of his almanacs:

> *If you would not be forgotten*
> *As soon as you are dead and rotten,*
> *Either write things worth reading*
> *Or do things worth the writing.*

Benjamin Franklin did both. Everything he wrote is worth reading, and everything he did has become part of the fabric of American history and of Western civilization.

CHAPTER V   The Peace Convention

of February 1861

🙐

Now that we are in the midst of Civil War celebrations,
it may be profitable to direct our attention from the
fighting which seems chiefly to interest the public, and
take a new look at a sincere last-minute effort to prevent
the war. The best known of these efforts are the Crittenden Compromise propositions, which Senator John J.
Crittenden of Kentucky worked on from December 1860
to February 1861. These, and their fate in Congress, have
been described at great length by James Ford Rhodes,
J. G. Randall, Allan Nevins, and other historians. But a
second, and in my opinion more important, effort to prevent the Civil War was the Peace Convention of delegates
from twenty-one states which met at Washington during
February 1861.[1]

---

[1] The stenographic notes of the Convention were printed by its
secretary, Lucius E. Chittenden of Vermont, as *A Report of the Debates
and Proceedings in the Secret Sessions of the Conference Convention,
for Proposing Amendments to the Constitution of the United States*
(New York, 1864). Chittenden also writes of the Convention in his
Recollections of President Lincoln (New York, 1904 ed.), and Governor
Boutwell in his *Reminiscences of Sixty Years,* I (New York, 1902). Of

This convention was summoned by invitation of the General Assembly of Virginia on January 19, 1861. The Crittenden Compromise proposals were encountering heavy weather in Congress, and it was hoped that a convention of the states could give these, or similar measures, authoritative support. Congress was unable to give compromise measures its undivided attention, and a convention could. And state governors, judges, and businessmen could be chosen to a convention and give it a broader base in the country.

In the Virginia resolution calling the Peace Convention, the Assembly declares its "deliberate opinion" to be "that unless the unhappy controversy which now divides the States of this confederacy, shall be satisfactorily adjusted, a permanent dissolution of Union is inevitable," and that this invitation to all the states is "a final effort to restore the Union and the Constitution, in the spirit in which they were established by the fathers of the Republic."

Senator James M. Mason of Virginia, reporting this action to the United States Senate on January 28, 1861, declared that "Virginia has undertaken the office of mediating between the two great sections of the country . . . restoring the Union under guarantees and provisions that

---

the secondary accounts, J. F. Rhodes: *History of the United States*, III (New York, 1907 ed.), 305-8, is brief but judicious; J. G. Randall: *Civil War and Reconstruction* (Boston, 1937), pp. 204-6, hews to the usual line, placing the onus of the Convention's failure on the Republicans. Allan Nevins: *Emergence of Lincoln*, II (New York, 1950), 411-12, has nothing new to say about it. Carl Sandburg: *Abraham Lincoln: The War Years*, I (New York, 1942 ed.), 85-90, is fair, but plays the "tired old men" theme.

might be satisfactory to both." He hoped that the Convention's proposals might "even win back" the six states which had already seceded; but warned that any attempt to coerce them would lead to war.

The Virginia Assembly, to give its proposal added weight, appointed a distinguished delegation, headed by ex-President John Tyler. Other members were William Cabell Rives, a courtly elder statesman, who had read law under Thomas Jefferson and represented the United States at the courts of Louis Philippe and Napoleon III, and James A. Seddon, a forty-five-year-old Richmond lawyer who later became Secretary of War of the Southern Confederacy. As such, he was described by his subordinate Jones, the gossipy "Rebel Clerk," as sallow and cadaverous, resembling "an exhumed corpse after a month's interment." The other Virginia members were George W. Summers of the western part of the state, and Judge John W. Brockenbrough of the federal district court.

Inviting all the states to be represented was not to John Tyler's liking. What he wanted was a convention of the slave states which had not seceded—North Carolina, Virginia, Maryland, Delaware, Kentucky, Tennessee, Arkansas, and Missouri. He had no hope or expectation of persuading the seceded states to return to the Union, but he felt that a convention limited to slave states which had not seceded could draw up a series of constitutional amendments protecting Southern rights as an ultimatum to the free states: i.e., a set of amendments the acceptance of which by the free states would prevent the border slave states from seceding. He knew that the seceded states would not accept membership in the Convention, which without them would have a Northern majority; and, as the Northern states would probably be represented by Republicans, that would hamstring his strategy. Whether or not John Tyler was a secessionist when the Convention opened, I do not know; but his words and actions prove that his heart was with the Southern Confederacy; and James Seddon, who did most of the talking for Virginia in the Convention, was an old Calhoun man and an avowed secessionist. Their actions remind one strongly of those of Timothy Pickering and John Lowell in respect to the Hartford Convention of 1814, with this important difference, that Pickering and Lowell were not members of the Hartford Convention.

The climate of opinion, when the Peace Convention opened, was favorable to compromise. Opinion in the North was in a state of flux. The secession of the cotton states had not been expected and was regarded with varied feelings. A notion was very prevalent that in electing Lincoln the North had gone too far. A meeting called by the Boston abolitionists on December 8, 1860, to celebrate the anniversary of John Brown's raid, was broken up by a "respectable" mob; and when, a few days later, Wendell Phillips addressed an abolitionist meeting, he had to be hustled home by a hundred policemen to escape the attentions of another mob. On February 12, 1861, a monster petition from 182 Massachusetts towns and cities in favor of the Crittenden Compromise, engrossed on a roll three feet wide and as big around as a cartwheel, containing 22,313 signatures, was rolled into the House of Representatives. Equally impressive petitions from other Northern states were brought in; two from New York City contained 63,000 signatures. Rhode Island had repealed, and Massachusetts did repeal in March, their personal liberty laws protecting fugitive slaves, which had given great offense to the South. Others were about to do so when the war broke out; Rhodes believed that all would have followed by May 1 "if it had been believed possible to save the Union in this way." During the winter, Senator Seward and Congressman Charles Francis Adams were doing everything in their power to appease Virginia and other border slave states, in order that Lincoln might at least be peacefully inaugurated on March 4.

Former Governor Boutwell, in his reminiscences published over forty years later, seems to bear out President Tyler's apprehensions that if Northern states were represented the Convention would come to no good. Boutwell regarded the whole affair as an attempt of secessionists to gain time. He declared that he and his colleagues would have accepted no compromise that did not include an abandonment of the doctrine of secession, an acknowledgment of the legality of Lincoln's election, and a declaration that loyal citizens must support the government. But the debates and the votes prove that only the Massachusetts delegation took this intransigent attitude. A large proportion of the Northern delegates were Democrats or former Whigs, strong for compromise, who voted for almost every measure that did not involve an invitation to acquire new slave territory.

James Gordon Bennett's mischievous New York *Herald* declared that the Northern delegates were "products of the grog shop" and members of "beaten and broken down factions"; but nothing could be further from the truth. Here are some of the more prominent. Maine was represented by Senators William Pitt Fessenden and Lot M. Morrill. New Hampshire sent Amos Tuck, one of the founders of the Republican party in the Granite State. Massachusetts sent former Governor George S. Boutwell, Francis Boardman Crowninshield, who had been Speaker of the House, John Murray Forbes, noted China merchant and railroad builder, and John Z. Goodrich of Stockbridge, a former congressman. New York sent a very distinguished delegation, evenly divided between Republicans and non-Republicans, including David Dudley Field, the eminent jurist; James S. Wadsworth of Geneseo; Erastus Corning, four times mayor of Albany, president of the New York Central Railroad, and Democratic representative in Congress; Francis Granger, fifty years out of Yale, and a leader of the conservative "Silver Gray" wing of the Whigs; and William E. Dodge, a wealthy dry-goods merchant, speculator, and philanthropist.

An amusing story about an encounter between Dodge and Lincoln is related by Carl Sandburg. Two days before Lincoln arrived in Washington, on February 23, he had no place to go. The committee on arrangements had reserved a suite at the National Hotel on Pennsylvania Avenue and Eighth Street. But Mrs. Lincoln put her foot down, refused to stay at the National Hotel because she had heard of an outbreak of ptomaine poisoning there in

1856, which had caused the death of several guests, including Governor Quitman of Mississippi, and had ruined the health of Senator Fessenden. The Willard Hotel, to which Mrs. Lincoln had no objection, was completely filled, and William E. Dodge had the best "parlor suite," on the second floor facing Pennsylvania Avenue. The committee persuaded him to relinquish it to the President-elect. But Dodge made Lincoln pay for this courtesy by forcing himself into the "parlor suite" and telling Lincoln that if he didn't favor a compromise "the grass shall grow in the streets of our commercial cities." Lincoln characteristically replied: "If it depends upon me, the grass shall not grow anywhere except in the fields and the meadows."

Rhode Island sent Chief Justice Samuel Ames, Governor William W. Hoppin, and Lieutenant Governor Samuel G. Arnold, the historian of his state; they seldom spoke and voted consistently with the Southern delegations. Connecticut sent Senator Roger S. Baldwin, Governor Chauncey F. Cleveland, and other solid citizens typical of the "Land of Steady Habits." New Jersey sent Governor Peter D. Vroom, Judge Joseph F. Randolph of the Supreme Court, Attorney General Frederick T. Frelinghuysen, and Commodore Robert F. Stockton, one of the most noted naval officers of his day. From Pennsylvania came Governor James Pollock, David Wilmot of Proviso fame, and Attorney General William M. Meredith.

Ohio sent Salmon P. Chase, the future Chief Justice, and the venerable Judge John C. Wright of her Supreme Court, who apparently was so overcome by the honor of being appointed temporary president at the opening session that he up and died. His funeral was held in the Convention's hall, and the oratorical tributes to his memory delivered on that occasion, followed by a procession from the hall to the Baltimore & Ohio depot, consumed an entire day. This episode seems to have confirmed a public impression that the Convention was composed of doddering old men; even Nevins calls the delegates "somewhat superannuated." This is not a fair statement. Naturally the governors and legislatures which appointed delegates chose solid citizens of poise and experience instead of political upstarts and "angry young men"; but that the Convention was not lacking in lustiness is proved by the service of many in the Civil War, the death in battle of at least four delegates,[2] and the political careers of many others after the war was over. John Tyler is also described by some of these writers as aged, emaciated, and tottering; but the portrait of him done that year shows that he still retained the air of an alert patrician, as in Tippecanoe-and-Tyler-too days. The letters of his wife, a Gardiner of Gardiner's Island, New York, indicate that she and her husband were well entertained during the Convention; Stephen A. Douglas even gave a ball for them. Boutwell was only forty-two years old; Seddon, who spoke for the Virginia delegation, was forty-five; and several of the members lived into the present century.

Indiana sent Caleb B. Smith, a former member of Congress who was about to be appointed Secretary of the Interior by President Lincoln; Illinois sent Judge Stephen

[2] Gen. Zollicoffer, killed at Battle of Fishing Creek, Ky.; Col. P. A. Hackleman of Indiana, killed at Corinth; Gen. James S. Wadsworth, killed in the Wilderness; Thomas Ruffin, died of wounds in Oct. 1863.

T. Logan, who had been Lincoln's law partner; Iowa was represented by Senator James W. Grimes, James Harlan, a future cabinet minister, and Congressman Samuel R. Curtis, a West Pointer and veteran of the Mexican War. As major general, U.S.A., Curtis became the hero of the Battle of Pea Ridge. Kansas sent her territorial chief justice, Thomas Ewing, Jr.

The border slave-state delegations were also well chosen, Delaware's alone consisting of nonentities, since apparently no members of the Du Pont family were available. From North Carolina came Governor and Senator David S. Reid, Congressman Thomas Ruffin, and Daniel M. Barringer, former United States minister to Spain. Tennessee sent the largest delegation, of twelve members, including Felix K. Zollicoffer, the future major general, C.S.A. Kentucky was represented by James B. Clay, son of the great Henry, Governor Charles E. Wickliffe, and James Guthrie, who had been Franklin Pierce's Secretary of the Treasury and in 1861 was president of the Louisville & Nashville Railroad; Guthrie turned out to be the great conciliator of the Convention. Missouri sent Alexander W. Doniphan, veteran of the Mexican War and a stalwart unionist. Maryland had a particularly distinguished delegation, headed by Reverdy Johnson, former Attorney General of the United States. It included Augustus W. Bradford, future governor of the state, and two representatives of old Maryland families: William T. Goldsborough and Benjamin C. Howard, reporter of the Supreme Court of the United States.

There were in all 133 delegates from 21 states. Some of the delegations were appointed by state governors;

others by legislatures; Maine and Iowa were represented
by their delegations in Congress. The only states not represented were California and Oregon, for reasons of time
and distance; the northwestern states, Michigan, Wis-
consin, and Minnesota, whose governors or legislatures
refused the invitation; the seven seceded states, who also
refused; and Arkansas and Louisiana, which were on the
brink of secession.

Michigan was one of three Northern states which could
have sent delegates but did not. After the Convention had
been in session a week, the two senators from Michigan
were persuaded to ask the state governor to appoint
delegates. Senator Zachary Chandler's letter to the governor said: "I hope you will send *stiff-backed* men or none.
The whole thing was gotten up against my judgment and
advice, and will end in thin smoke. . . . Some of the
manufacturing States think that a fight would be awful.
Without a little bloodletting this Union will not in my
estimation, be worth a rush." This letter leaked out, and
was flourished both in the Convention and the Senate
as proof of Republican duplicity and intractability. And
every secondary account of the Convention features the
Chandler letter as a reason for the Convention's failure
to accomplish anything. Actually, it seems to have had no
influence whatever, and Michigan never sent any delegates. Chandler represented only the radical Republican
line, which in the Convention was followed consistently
only by the Massachusetts delegation. Other Northern
delegates who were Republicans, such as Logan of Illinois,
Chase of Ohio, and Cleveland of Connecticut, were as
conciliatory as anyone in the Convention.

The joint resolutions of most of the state legislatures breathe a spirit of compromise. Those of the border slave states and New Jersey were the most favorable and enthusiastic. Those of the Northern states which had voted for Lincoln took a rather "show me" attitude—Ohio, typically, declared that she was "not prepared" to accept the compromises proposed by Virginia in the invitation, and felt that the Constitution of the United States "contains ample provisions within itself for the correction of all evils complained" of; yet respect for a sister state and "a sincere desire to have harmoniously adjusted all differences between us" have persuaded Ohio to send delegates. Indiana and Illinois passed similar resolves, Illinois adding that she considered a new federal convention to be the better way to harmonize sectional difficulties. Pennsylvania intimated that she was ready to accept a stronger fugitive slave law, and to unite with Virginia "in an earnest effort to restore the peace of the country." The General Court of Massachusetts passed a rather dry and noncommital resolution.

Let us briefly throw our minds back to that day, when Washington was a straggling mid-century American town of 75,000 people, of whom 11,000 were Negroes, and of them, 3,200 were slaves. Even at that, Washington was too big for its breeches, having grown fifty per cent in the last ten years. Apart from Major l'Enfant's plan, which promised well for the future, the city was completely lacking in distinction. Almost every street was unpaved, horse-drawn buses afforded the only public transportation, the only public buildings were the half-finished Capitol, the unenlarged White House, the Treasury, the Smith-

sonian, and the Corcoran (now called the Old Court of
Claims building) at Pennsylvania Avenue and Seventeenth
Street. State, Army, Navy, and Interior were housed in
two- and three-story brick buildings that have long since
disappeared. Everyone who was anybody lived in or near
Lafayette Square, or between it and cozy Georgetown.
The incomplete Washington monument, built up to only
one-third of its height, and the unfinished dome of the
Capitol, surmounted by an unsightly fringe of derricks,
seemed symbols of the mess of unfinished business that
the spineless Democratic administration had left for
Lincoln to tackle. Here is what young Henry Adams
thought of our nation's capital: "As in 1800 and 1850, so
in 1860, the same rude colony was camped in the same
forest, with the same unfinished Greek temples for work-
rooms, and sloughs for roads. The Government had an
air of social instability and incompleteness that went far
to support the right of secession in theory as in fact; . . .
secession was likely to be easy where there was so little to
secede from."

The Peace Convention met in Willard's Hall, an old
theater adjoining Willard's Hotel which the hotel had
acquired. The management placed the hall at the Convention's disposal free of charge, doubtless expecting to
profit by increased patronage of the nearby bar.

The Convention took itself very seriously. It adopted
a set of rules based on those of the Federal Convention
of 1787. These required voting by state units, nobody to
be allowed to speak more than twice on one question,
and sessions to be completely secret. Each session was

opened with prayer. Washington, then as now, was a very "leaky" place, and the Drew Pearsons of 1861 had no difficulty in obtaining the gist of what went on for insertion in their columns.

John Tyler, unanimously chosen president, made a gracious speech of acceptance, begging the delegates to prove themselves "worthy of the great occasion." A Committee of Fifteen, composed of one member from each of that number of states, with James Guthrie of Kentucky as chairman, was appointed to propose constitutional amendments as a basis of discussion. And on February 15, when the Committee of Fifteen reported, the Convention really got down to work.

By that time it was obvious that the Convention could no longer hope to restore "the Union as it was," only to prevent further disintegration. For on February 9 the Confederate States of America had been organized at Montgomery, Alabama, Jefferson Davis chosen President and Alexander H. Stephens Vice-President. On the 16th Davis reached Montgomery after making some twenty-five speeches en route from his home in Mississippi. Upon his arrival he declared that the time for compromise had passed, that Southern independence must be maintained, even at the cost of civil war, and that no propositions for a reconstruction of the Union would be entertained.

Here is what the Committee of Fifteen reported in the way of constitutional amendments:

1. The amendment to which Senator Crittenden of Kentucky had already attached his name, extending the

old Missouri Compromise line, 36° 30', to the California boundary. North of it, slavery to be prohibited, south of it, slavery to be permitted, when under territorial government; states to be admitted from either side of the line with or without slavery as their respective constitutions might determine. This amendment to be irrepealable by subsequent amendment without unanimous consent of the states.

2. No new territory to be acquired by the United States, except by treaty, which "treaty shall be ratified by four-fifths of all members of the Senate." This to be similarly irrepealable except by unanimous consent.

3. The "Never-never" Amendment, as I shall call it for short. Congress shall never abolish, regulate, or control, nor shall any subsequent amendment ever abolish, regulate, or control slavery in any state or territory of the United States, or in the District of Columbia without the consent of Maryland; or even, in that event, to prevent people from slave states bringing slaves into Washington, or to interfere with the interstate slave trade by land or sea.

4. The fugitive slave clause of the Constitution (Article IV, Section ii, §3) to be enforced, against state personal liberty laws.

5. The foreign slave trade to be forever prohibited.

6. In addition to all the above being irrepealable, Article I, Section ii, §3, on the federal ratio of representation, will be irrepealable by future amendment, except by unanimous consent.

7. Congress to provide for compensation to slave-

owners, the return of whose fugitive slaves is prevented by violence.

That was quite a mouthful for the Northern members of the committee to swallow; and three of them dissented. Roger Baldwin of Connecticut reported as a substitute that Congress summon a full and complete constitutional convention, as the legislature of Kentucky had already proposed. David Dudley Field and Francis B. Crowninshield, who were not on the committee, promptly expressed their dissent from the committee's report.

The report was equally unsatisfactory to the Virginia delegation, but from an opposite point of view. The Virginia General Assembly, in issuing the call to the Convention, had resolved that the Crittenden Compromise, extending the 36° 30′ line to California, would be acceptable only if it protected slavery in all territory "now held or hereafter acquired" south of this line. Those three words "or hereafter acquired" were really Virginia's ultimatum. They meant, as everyone knew, that slavery could be extended into any future territory, such as Cuba, the northern tier of Mexican states, or Nicaragua, that might be acquired by purchase, filibustering, or war. That demand, as we shall see, was absolutely and completely inacceptable to the Northern states; but the Virginia delegation would accept nothing less. James Seddon said so, frankly, to Boutwell, when that head of the Massachusetts delegation called on him—"We must have new lands." There must have been many unrecorded conversations of this kind among the delegates, and between

them and other politicians in Washington. New friendships were made across the borders, and after the war
was over Boutwell bestirred himself to have Seddon's
political disabilities as a "rebel" removed.

The rigidity of the Virginia attitude became evident
when Seddon on February 15 brought in a set of substitute
propositions. These, he said, if incorporated as constitutional amendments, would make Virginia feel safe within
the Union. Here they are, in brief:

1. The 36° 30′ extension, with the "hereafter acquired"
clause.

2. Federal officials within a state to be removed by the
President, upon demand of a majority of the senators of
either section. I.e., if the objectionable official were in a
slave state, a resolution of no confidence by a majority of
slave-state senators would be sufficient to throw him out.
This extraordinary proposal, which was John Tyler's bright
idea, came from the fear that Lincoln would appoint
"Black Republican" marshals and district attorneys in
the South.

3. Explicit recognition of the right of secession, and
prohibition against any form of coercion of a seceded
state.

These propositions, significant as they were, never
came to a vote.

By February 16 the Convention realized that time was
running short. Governor Wickliffe observed that the
Thirty-sixth Congress would end on March 4, and nothing
the Convention might recommend would be valid unless

adopted by Congress. He proposed to limit all speeches to thirty minutes. Seddon opposed, and the motion was not carried. But one concession was made to the flight of time—the Convention decided to start sessions at 11 a.m. instead of noon.

Samuel R. Curtis of Iowa challenged Seddon on the right of secession. "If any State has the right to go out of the Union at its own volition, then this Government . . . is not worth the trouble of preserving. . . . The Government is one of love and affection, it is true, but it is also one of strength and power. Where was there ever a more indulgent people than ours? Our forts have been taken, our flag has been fired upon, our property seized, and as yet nothing has been done. But . . . beware, gentlemen, how you force them further."

Reverdy Johnson of Maryland now made an eloquent speech in favor of the 36° 30′ extension, the one amendment that he considered essential to keep the border slave states in the Union. He pointed out that this amendment, restoring the old Missouri Compromise line, would be a Southern concession, since the Supreme Court had declared slavery to be legal in all United States territories north of the line; and since, according to the proposed amendment, territories even south of the line might enter the Union as free states if they chose. He did not allude to the "hereafter acquired" clause; and Seddon of Virginia, in reply, picked him up on that. Virginia, said Seddon, "insists on the provision for future territory. She and her sister States plant themselves upon it." He also demanded fresh guarantees for the protection of slave property. "We hold our *property*, yes, *our property in slaves*, as rightful and as honorable as any property to be found in the broad expanse between ocean and ocean," said this spokesman for Virginia. It is a matter of honor, "the soul of nations." Without special protection to our property, "we are a dishonored people." "We feel that in the existence, the perpetuity [in slavery, presumably], the protection of the African race, we have a mission to perform, and . . . a duty." He proceeded to glorify the condition of the slaves in the South, as compared with that of the emancipated Negroes in Haiti and Jamaica. He declared that the pernicious doctrine of abolition originated in England, with the express purpose of destroying the American Union, and that the John Brown raid was the logical result of these efforts. He denounced the Republican party as based on "greed of office and power," and animated by "the ruling idea" of using "the whole power of the administration . . . for the final extinction of slavery." And he concluded with an ill-concealed threat that if Virginians were not given the "guarantees which will give them actual power instead of mere paper rights," the state convention, then sitting at Richmond, would vote for secession.

I wish that some of our evasive historians, our mufflers of great passionate issues, who are trying to persuade the American public that Negro slavery had nothing to do with the Civil War, would read the debates in this Peace Convention. There is no suggestion in any of the Southern delegates' speeches of any grievance against the North, or against the Republican party, other than hostility to slavery. Tariff, internal improvements, all those trumped-up issues which were the grist of Confederate propaganda then, and since, were never even mentioned. It is interesting to note that while Seddon was orating at Washington, H. L. Benning of Georgia appeared before the Virginia Convention at Richmond as envoy of the Confederate States, offering Virginia, if she would join the Southern Confederacy, to pass a protective tariff and build up manufacturing to make her "the New England of the South." States' rights are indeed frequently mentioned in the Convention debates, but only as a justification for preserving slavery.

Former Governor Boutwell was selected by the Massachusetts delegation and by the Republicans of the New York delegation to reply to Seddon. "Massachusetts," he observed, "has made war upon slavery wherever she had a right to do it; but much as she *abhors* the institution, she would sacrifice anything rather than assail it when she has not the right to assail it"—i.e., in the states that have it. A President has been elected "in a legal and constitutional way." Do the Southern gentlemen mean to suggest that his inauguration will not be permitted unless these guarantees to slavery be adopted? If the Union "cannot be preserved . . . without these new guarantees for slavery," he believes "that the Union is not worth preserving." He is ready to admit that, owing to the Dred Scott decision, slavery now legally exists in all United States territories. And he disapproves all restriction on the acquisition of new territory; "the Canadas" may wish to join the United States. He does not think that the Northern states will ever "consent to these new endorsements of an institution which they do not like, which they believe to be injurious to the best interests of the Republic. . . . But the North will never consent to the separation of the States. If the South persists in the course on which she has entered we shall march our armies to the Gulf of Mexico, or you will march yours to the Great Lakes. There can be no peaceful separation." Boutwell later remembered that when he said this, tears started from the eyes of William Cabell Rives.

Boutwell's statement that Massachusetts "abhors" slavery stirred up bad blood, which shows how far the South had moved in the previous generation. Washington detested slavery, Jefferson abhorred slavery, and George Mason in the Federal Convention denounced slavery; but, by 1860, for anyone to admit that he or his state "abhorred" slavery was an argument for secession. Boutwell himself records that it "grieved" the Southern members "sorely" and that some tried to persuade him "to retract or qualify it." Boutwell would better have said that Massachusetts "regrets" slavery—not that it made any difference in the end.

James Guthrie followed with a conciliatory speech. This Kentuckian, one of the few members of the Convention who was more businessman than politician, showed the nearest approach to statesmanship of any, except possibly Reverdy Johnson of Maryland. Governor Cleveland of Connecticut begged for an end to sectional recriminations. "Let us be gentle and pleasant. Let us love one another. Let us not try to find out who is the smartest or keenest. Let us vote soon, and without any feeling or any quarrelling."

An effort was now made on motion of George Davis of North Carolina to cut down the length of speeches to ten minutes, and to bring the proposed amendments to a vote. This proposal to choke off the flow of oratory, so contrary to the habits of that era, was vigorously opposed. William E. Dodge protested that he wished "to speak for the commercial interests of the country," and "cannot do them justice in ten minutes." The debate whether or not to apply the snuffer consumed an entire day, during which Commodore Stockton gave a speech that must have taken at least an hour to deliver. He invoked the memory of Quintus Curtius (meaning, I suppose, the legendary Marcus Curtius who leaped into the chasm to save Rome), reviewed the English Civil War and the entire expanse of American history, and predicted that "the use of the sword to conquer secession" was an infatuation—"Why, you cannot force New Jersey alone!"[3] The venerable Francis Granger of New York delivered a long and conciliatory speech in favor of the amendments, concluding with an eloquent plea for union. William Cabell Rives of Virginia followed, declaring: "I condemn the secession of States. I am not here to justify it. I detest it. But the great fact is still before us. . . . With this fact the nation must deal. . . . Coercion is not a word to be used in this connection. There must be negotiation. Virginia presents

[3] New Jersey, last of the Northern states to start emancipation of the slaves, still had eighteen slaves in 1860, and the sympathetic attitude of this delegation raised an expectation that she might join the Southern Confederacy if Maryland and Delaware did.

herself as a mediator to bring back those who have left us." Rives was the only delegate who clung to the hope of bringing the "wayward sisters" back; for the others, it was only a question of finding guarantees to prevent the other slave states from joining them. Rives, in reply to Boutwell's "abhorrence" of slavery, taunted him with the charge that Massachusetts had "fastened" slavery on the South against its will, in order to profit from the slave trade—a hoary myth still widely believed in the South.

Governor Morrill of Maine tried to bring the Convention back to reality by asking: "What will Virginia do? How does Virginia stand? She to-day holds the keys of peace or war. . . . She undertakes to dictate the terms upon which the Union is to be preserved. What will satisfy her?" Seddon replied: "Virginia *will not permit coercion*," but he would not be drawn into giving an opinion as to whether or not his proposed amendments would keep her in the Union. George W. Summers of the Virginia delegation, who represented Kanawha County, accepted the challenge from Down East, and gave it as his opinion that Virginia would accept the amendments proposed by the committee as satisfactory; he made a touching plea to the New England members "not to refuse us the little boon we ask, when the consequences of that refusal must be so awful." He declared he would *"never give up the Union*," nor did he. After making an eloquent plea for union in the Virginia Convention at Richmond, George Summers helped to organize the state of West Virginia.

The motion to limit speeches to ten minutes did not

come up until next day, when it was defeated; and the rumble of high-caliber oratory was resumed.

Of all the speeches made before the final vote, the only one that said anything new, or anything old in a new way, was by David Dudley Field of New York. This speech confirms what I have been told by a justice of the Supreme Court of the United States, that Field was one of the greatest of American jurists, in a class with Chancellor Kent and Judge Story. He pointed out, on the authority of President Buchanan, that Congress had never passed a law concerning slavery that the South thought unconstitutional, except the Missouri Compromise, which had been repealed. President-elect Lincoln has given every assurance that the Republican administration will not interfere with slavery in the States. "Can you not be satisfied with that? No. You propose these amendments in advance. You insist upon them. . . . But, gentlemen of the South, what reasons do you give for entering upon this hasty, this precipitate action? You say it is the prevailing sense of insecurity, the anxiety, the apprehension you feel lest something unlawful . . . may be done. Yet the gentleman from Virginia (Mr. Seddon) tells us that Virginia is able to protect all who reside within her limits, and that she will do so at all hazards. Why not tell us the truth outright? . . . You are determined to prevent the agitation of the subject. . . . You have called us here to prevent future discussion of . . . slavery. It is *that* you fear —it is *that* you would avoid—discussion in Congress—in the State Legislatures—in the newspapers—in popular assemblies." And he went on to say that the proposed amendments would not accomplish this end; rather they, especially the one to enforce the fugitive slave law, would be "throwing a lighted firebrand . . . into every county, city, and village" in the land. He declared: "I would sacrifice all I have; lay down my life for the Union. But I will not give these guarantees to slavery." And, by way of peroration, he closed with the famous passage from Longfellow's "Launching of the Ship."

Field certainly went to the root of the matter, but that was not the way to conciliate. Judge Thomas White of the Pennsylvania delegation followed him with a plea for speedy action in favor of the proposed amendments, which he regarded as advantageous to the North. Frelinghuysen of New Jersey also spoke in favor of them. William E. Dodge finally got his chance to speak "as a plain merchant" for the businessmen of New York City. He allowed that he was "accustomed to the trials, vexations, cares, and responsibilities of business," but this situation was worse than anything he had experienced: last night he "could not close" his "eyes in slumber" because of the "certain and inevitable ruin" that is threatening business. In New York City, Baltimore, Philadelphia, and Boston, business is stagnant; goods are not moving from the shelves, customers are scarce, shop clerks "sit around in idleness reading the newspapers"; in New England "the noise of the loom, the rattle of the shuttle" have ceased, and all because of sectional misunderstanding. The New England delegates misunderstood their own people in opposing Mr. Seddon's propositions. The Yankees "are a shrewd and calculating as well as an enterprising people";

they will go for these amendments if they understand the necessity of them to save their section from ruin.

And so the debate went on, with amendments and counter-amendments. There was very little sectional re-crimination—far less than in congressional debates, because the delegates were there to find a compromise, and because they had no audience other than themselves. On February 23 the delegates were received by President Lincoln in the parlor suite relinquished by Mr. Dodge; and William Cabell Rives, at least, was impressed. He wrote home that this President-elect was a real man, who was not going to be run by any abolitionist clique and that he could find no fault with his views as then expressed.

On February 26 matters finally came to a head. Seddon, who did almost all the speaking for the Virginia delegation, brought in a fresh set of proposed amendments, which, he said, embodied the Crittenden resolutions, with such alterations as the Virginia delegation had been "instructed to insist upon." They were as follows:

1. Extension of the 36° 30′ line, with the "hereafter acquired" words inserted, that would extend slavery to future acquisitions south of the line.

2. and 3. The "Never-never" Amendment about slavery in the states, and in the District of Columbia.

4. Congress to have no power to interfere with the domestic slave trade, and the right of transit of slaves through free states to be protected.

5. Compensation to owners of fugitive slaves when their return has been prevented by state law or force.

6. All the above amendments, and also Article I, Section ii, §3, to be irrepealable except by unanimous consent of the states.

7. People of Negro blood to be ineligible for the franchise, whether federal, state, or municipal.

To these proposed amendments were added resolutions as a guide to congressional and state action:

1. The states are "respectfully and earnestly" recommended to repeal their personal liberty laws.

2. The Fugitive Slave Act to be strengthened and enforced.

3. Laws for the suppression of the African slave trade to be made more effectual.

The Seddon substitutes were emphatically rejected, only Virginia, North Carolina, Kentucky, and Missouri voting for them. Clay of Kentucky then brought in a somewhat modified set of Seddon resolves, which was defeated by a similar vote, only Tennessee joining the four states in favor.

Amos Tuck of New Hampshire now brought in a completely different set of resolutions, embodying the "Never-never" Amendment, plus non-recognition of the right of secession. This was eloquently argued for by Salmon P. Chase. But it received the votes of nine states only—all Northern—with eleven states, including New Jersey, Ohio, Pennsylvania, and Rhode Island, against.

It was clear that the Convention was deadlocked. There was a general wringing of hands. Commodore Stockton again evoked the history of ancient Rome. "Alas!

Is there no Curtius here" to throw himself into the chasm and sacrifice his life to save his country?

Well, there was—just one; James Guthrie of Kentucky, and it was his propositions, amended, which came up for the final vote on February 26–27:

1. The Crittenden 36° 30′ amendment. When this came to a vote it was defeated, eight states to eleven, and not by sectional alignment. Four free states—New Jersey, Ohio, Pennsylvania, and Rhode Island—voted for it; three slave states—Virginia, North Carolina, and Missouri—helped defeat it, obviously because it lacked the "hereafter acquired" clause.

This was the crisis of the Convention. The border-state men "were sorely disappointed, and some of them wept like children," remembered Boutwell. "The disagreeable silence which followed the announcement of the vote, was broken by Mr. Francis Granger," who counseled moderation and moved to reconsider.[4] His motion was adopted, fourteen states to five, and Guthrie brought up the amendment again next morning, when it was adopted, nine states to eight. Illinois was the state that changed its vote in favor; a deadlock in the New York and Missouri delegations reduced the opposing states to eight.

Thus, the 36° 30′ extension, without the "hereafter acquired" clause, was adopted.

The next proposition to come to a vote, No. 2, was to the effect that no new territory could be acquired

---

[4] Boutwell: *Reminiscences*, I, 274. Boutwell said that the reconsideration was attributed to the influence of Lincoln, but there is no evidence that he intervened in any way in the deliberations of the Convention.

without the concurrence of a majority of the senators from the slave states, and a majority of those of the free states. This was adopted, eleven states to eight, all the slave-state delegations except North Carolina's voting for it; five New England states, Illinois, and Iowa against it.

3. The "Never-never" Amendment, as to slavery in the states, or the District of Columbia, or interfering with the domestic slave trade. Adopted, twelve states to seven; only five New England states, Indiana, and Iowa in the minority.

4. Enforcing the fugitive slave clause of the Constitution, Article IV, Section ii, §3. Adopted, fifteen states to four; Maine, Massachusetts, New Hampshire, and Iowa in the minority.

5. Foreign slave trade forever prohibited, and the prohibition extended to "coolies" and contract labor. Adopted, sixteen states to five; Virginia, North Carolina, Iowa, Maine, and Massachusetts in the minority.

6. The above amendments Nos. 1, 3, and 5, plus the federal ratio clause (Article I, Section ii, §3) and the fugitive slave clause (Article IV, Section ii, §3) of the Constitution to be irrepealable save by unanimous consent of all the states. Passed, eleven states to nine. Virginia, North Carolina, Indiana, Iowa, and five New England states constituted the minority.

7. Compensation for fugitive slaves. Passed, twelve states to seven; Virginia, North Carolina, Missouri, Iowa, and three New England states in the minority.

Obviously, this was far from a clean-cut vote. The New York delegation was divided fifty-fifty, between its

Republican and non-Republican members, on every one of the seven propositions. Kansas was divided on three. Virginia's vote was cast by a three-to-two majority within her delegation. And after every vote several members spoke up dissociating themselves from the vote of their respective states. But the seven propositions were adopted by the Convention, and by it presented as Amendment XIII to the Constitution, to the Thirty-sixth Congress, which had but a few more days of life.

Note that the Maine, Massachusetts, and Iowa delegations voted against everything, and that they were joined by New Hampshire, Vermont, and Connecticut in voting against the 36° 30′ amendment, the "Never-never" Amendment, and the one making these amendments irrepealable. If these delegations accurately represented the sentiment of their states, there was little chance of getting the seven proposed amendments adopted.

But the really significant thing in the vote is that of Virginia. Her delegation, supported except in one instance by that of North Carolina, voted against four of the seven propositions, including the crucial 36° 30′ one. Since Virginia had initiated the Convention, and since the principal object of it was to give Virginia and the other border states guarantees which would enable their union men to triumph over the secessionists, this negative attitude of the Virginia delegation meant that the Convention's labors were in vain.

President Tyler himself immediately made this clear. On February 28, the day after the Convention adjourned, he made a public speech from the steps of the Exchange Hotel at Richmond openly advocating the secession of his state. Seddon did likewise, and both took seats in the Virginia Convention and assumed leadership of the secessionists. Summers alone of the Virginia delegation maintained a firm opposition to secession.

The surprising thing in the vote is the unanimous affirmative of all slave states except North Carolina for the concurrent majority provision for annexing new territory; for it would have given a majority of free-state senators the right to block the annexation of Cuba or other slave territory to the southward. Possibly Governor Boutwell's insinuation of a future annexation of Canada, which would have meant at least four new free states, prompted this vote.

The fate of the Convention's amendments in the Senate, to which they were presented on February 27, is equally significant. Senator Crittenden, "the Nestor of the Senate," who had represented Kentucky there at intervals for forty-four years, promptly accepted the proposed Amendment XIII as a substitute for the propositions for which he had been laboring since Lincoln's election. But the amendment was strongly opposed by both senators from Virginia, Mason and Hunter.

Senator Seward of New York proposed to substitute a call for a new federal constitutional convention. Senator Hunter endeavored in vain to bring back the "hereafter acquired" proviso in the 36° 30' section. The whole subject was thrashed out in the Senate on that and the next few days, and also in the House.

The only part of the Peace Convention's recommendation to survive the 4th of March was the "Never-never"

Amendment, forever protecting slavery in the states and the District of Columbia from congressional interference. The Republicans were willing to accept this, since in the Chicago platform of 1860 they had disclaimed any right or intention to interfere with slavery in the states, and President Lincoln had repeatedly stated that he had no objection to it. Lincoln made a clean-cut distinction between assurance and appeasement. He was willing to give the South assurance that his party would not meddle with slavery in the states, but he felt that appeasement of the South on slavery extension and fugitive slaves, which had been actively pursued by the Democratic party since 1850, had been a failure, and that his election was the result of a popular protest against it. So he would support no amendment that allowed further extension of slavery.

The "Never-never" Amendment, in substantially the same form in which it issued from the Peace Convention, was adopted on February 28 by the House of Representatives by a vote of 133 to 65 (Charles Francis Adams and many other Republicans voting in favor) and by the Senate by 24 to 12—the exact constitutional majority of two-thirds—on March 3, 1861. The same day it received the unnecessary approval of President Buchanan. This amendment was actually ratified by three states—by Ohio on May 13, 1861, Maryland on January 10, 1862, and Illinois on February 14, 1862.

In conclusion, the Peace Convention was held as a result of a sincere desire on the part of the Virginia General Assembly, not only to find guarantees for slavery where it existed, and so stifle the secession movement, but also to woo the seceded states back into the Union. Although the second object was seen to be irrealizable a few days after the Convention met, the first was persisted in through almost three weeks of committee work and debate. It failed because the Virginia delegation, dominated by President Tyler and Seddon, refused to abate two demands made at the very start. The first was to the effect that the 36° 30′ compromise line between freedom and slavery in the territories must allow for acquiring new slave territory to the southward. The second was a recognition of the right of secession. Virginia did obtain approval by the Convention of the "Never-never" Amendment, of the dual provision for acquiring new territory, and of a stronger fugitive slave law; but these did not satisfy her leading public men as effective guarantees.

I agree with James Ford Rhodes, that "the historical significance of the Peace Convention consists in the evidence it affords of the attachment of the border slave States to the Union, and the lingering hope of readjustment in North Carolina and Tennessee." But was not the conflict, by that time, irrepressible? Could anything short of a change of heart in the South, to regard slavery as something to be eventually liquidated, or on the part of the North, wholeheartedly to suppress criticism of slavery, have prevented the Civil War? President Lincoln and the Republicans had been given a clear mandate to allow no further extension of slave territory. They were willing to admit new slave states south of the old 36° 30′ line, since the Dred Scott decision had already declared slavery to be legal in that region. They were willing to accept the "Never-never" Amendment; but beyond that, as Lincoln insisted, they held firm.[5]

James B. McKean of Saratoga Springs, New York, a member of Congress not otherwise known to fame, hit the nail on the head when, discussing the 36° 30′ amendment with the "hereafter acquired" clause, he ironically proposed a different amendment:

Whenever a party shall be beaten in an election for President and Vice President, such party may rebel and take up arms, and, unless the successful shall adopt as its own the principles of the defeated party, and consent to such amendments of the Constitution as the latter party shall dictate, then, in such case, the Union shall be at an end.[6]

Governor Boutwell was no compromiser, and in his reminiscences he states why. "Conspirators are never disposed to make terms with the party against whom their conspiracy is aimed, until the conspiracy has failed." Note how aptly this applies to the negotiations with Hitler before World War II. I would not attach the invidious term "conspiracy" to the Southern secessionists, who had been working in the open for years, or compare the honorable Jefferson Davis to Adolf Hitler. But it seems clear, after a century has elapsed, that what Stephen Vincent

[5] See the interesting discussion in Nevins: *Emergence of Lincoln*, II, 407–9, and Martin Duberman: *Charles Francis Adams* (Boston, 1961), pp. 232–43, of Adams's attempts to appease the South by admitting New Mexico as a slave state.

[6] *Congressional Globe*, 36th Cong., 2nd Sess., Pt. II, Appendix, p. 222. Andrew C. McLaughlin quoted this in his review of Rhodes's Vol. III in *American Historical Review*, I (1896), 368, but incorrectly named the speaker McLean.

Benét called the "purple dream" of an empire based on slavery, extending into the Caribbean, was so enticing, and so apparently attainable, that no manner of appeasement on the part of the free states and the Republican party could have stopped the Southern Confederacy in 1861. And it is transparently clear that nothing short of acquiescence in this dismemberment of the Union could have prevented the secession of Virginia.

Chapter VI   The Battle off Samar

October 25, 1944

❧

One of the strangest incidents in this or any other modern war occurred on October 25, 1944, forty miles off the Philippine island of Samar, about fifteen minutes after sunrise. An escort carrier group known by its code name, "Taffy 3," under Rear Admiral Clifton Sprague in U.S.S. *Fanshaw Bay*, having launched routine patrols to cover the ships in Leyte Gulf, had secured from Battle Quarters. The deck crews were eating breakfast. At 0645 lookouts observed antiaircraft fire to the northward. What could that possibly be? At 0646 the flagship's radar screen showed something odd. One minute later the pilot of a plane on antisubmarine patrol reported that he was being fired upon by a force of battleships, cruisers, and destroyers at a position some twenty miles distant. "Check identification!" yelled Admiral Sprague to air plot. But before verification of this astonishing contact could be obtained, sailors on lookout sighted the unmistakable tall masts of Japanese battleships and cruisers pricking up over the northwestern horizon. At 0648 these ships opened fire, and a minute later splashes from their shells began rising all around Taffy 3.

It was Admiral Kurita's powerful Center Force of the Japanese Combined Fleet. He was every bit as surprised as Sprague. He thought he had run smack into Mitscher's Task Force 38, the big fleet carriers.

How could this formidable fleet have covered 125 to 150 miles from inside San Bernardino Strait, down along the ocean shore of Samar, in the last seven hours, undetected by ship, search plane, or coast watcher?

Admiral Halsey had been informed by a night-search plane from *Independence* that Kurita's Center Force would sortie from San Bernardino Strait. Sightings on it heading that way reached the Admiral as late as 2120, October 24. But he simply did not care. Estimating that his carrier pilots' exaggerated reports of their sinkings in the Battle of the Sibuyan Sea that day were correct, he assumed that Center Force "could no longer be considered a serious menace to Seventh Fleet," in or outside Leyte Gulf, and did not even warn Admiral Kinkaid, the commander of that fleet, to watch out. By the time Halsey received the night-sighting reports, his Third Fleet—less McCain's task group, which he had sent south to fuel— was hightailing north, hellbent after Ozawa's Northern Force. That was exactly what the Japanese wanted it to do. Halsey might have spared one carrier group and Admiral Lee's Battle Line (*New Jersey, Iowa, Washington, Massachusetts, Alabama*) to guard San Bernardino Strait; but he left not even a picket destroyer. That is why Kurita's Center Force was able to debouch unseen into

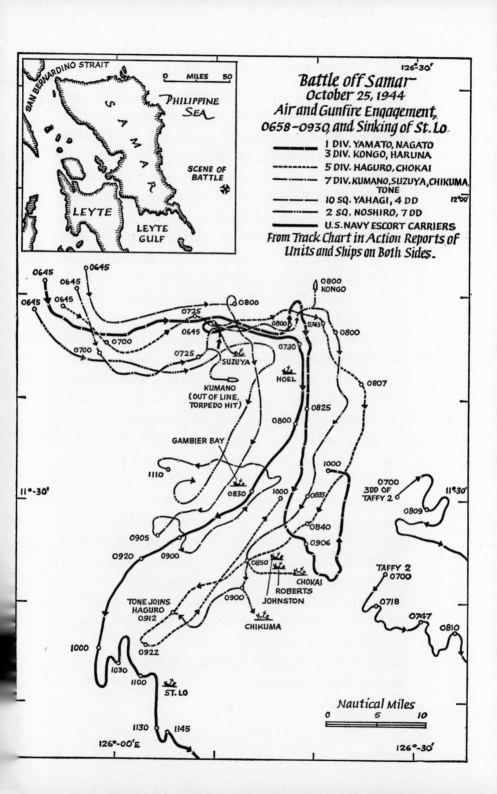

Battle off Samar
October 25, 1944
Air and Gunfire Engagement,
0658-0930, and Sinking of St. Lo.

the Philippine Sea at 0030, October 25, and steam south unseen off the Samar shore, until intercepted by Clifton Sprague's escort carriers. And that is why Taffy 3, composed of six escort carriers with no guns bigger than 5-inch, screened by three destroyers and four destroyer escorts, had to fight Kurita's four battleships, six heavy cruisers, and numerous destroyers.

Taffy 3 was supported by the aircraft of two other groups of nearly the same strength: Rear Admiral Thomas L. Sprague's Taffy 1, which was operating well to the southward, off Mindanao; and Rear Admiral Felix B. Stump's Taffy 2, then off the entrance to Leyte Gulf. The total plane complement of these 16 carriers was 235 fighter planes (Hellcats and Wildcats) and 143 Avenger torpedo planes; and it was they, in addition to Clifton Sprague's skillful tactics, and the intrepid attacks by his screen, which enabled him to win this battle against an overwhelming surface and gunfire superiority. But few of these planes were available at the moment of surprise. Taffy 1 had already launched a strike group to pursue Japanese ships fleeing down Surigao Strait; all carriers had launched planes for routine patrol, or for odd jobs such as delivering cans of fresh water to the troops on Leyte.

The Battle off Samar, thus unexpectedly joined at 0648, was the most remarkable of the Pacific war, since the tactics had to be improvised. Prewar training prepared the United States Navy to fight battles such as Surigao Strait; but there was no preparation, no doctrine, for a force of "baby flattops" fighting a battle fleet such as Kurita's. Their training was all for supporting amphibious operations by strikes and combat air and antisubmarine patrols, not for bearing the brunt of a major battle. Rear Admiral Clifton A. F. Sprague, known as "Ziggy" in the Navy, an able and conscientious officer forty-eight years old, had commanded fleet carrier *Wasp* in the Battle of the Philippine Sea, but now he faced a unique challenge.

Weather gave the escort carriers their first break. Wind blew from the eastern quadrant, permitting them to steer away from the enemy while launching planes, and rain squalls afforded occasional cover. Clifton Sprague, knowing very well what a pickle he was in, acted with cool and correct decision. He turned Taffy 3 due east, upped speed to the flattop maximum of 17½ knots, ordered every plane to be launched and to attack, and broadcast an urgent plea for assistance. Admirals Tom Sprague and Felix Stump responded quickly; but Taffy 1 lay 130 miles distant; could its planes get there in time?

Kurita fumbled from the moment the battle joined. His staff told him that the escort carriers were fleet carriers, the destroyers cruisers, and the destroyer escorts destroyers. At the moment of impact, he was changing the disposition of Center Force from cruising to anti-aircraft formation. He should promptly have formed battle line with his fast, powerful ships and committed light forces to torpedo attack. Instead, he ordered General Attack—every ship for itself—which threw his force into confusion and made the battle a helter-skelter affair, ships committed piecemeal and defeated piecemeal, just as the Japanese Army was wont to do ashore.

Clifton Sprague formed his six carriers into a ragged

circle 2,500 yards in diameter, his screen patrolling outside the engaged sector, as Japanese salvos edged closer and closer. At 0706, to quote his Action Report: "The enemy was closing with disconcerting rapidity and the volume and accuracy of fire was increasing. At this point it did not appear that any of our ships could survive another five minutes of the heavy-caliber fire being received." His task unit being faced by "the ultimate in desperate circumstances," he saw that counteraction was urgently required. He ordered all his escorts to make a torpedo attack. And, also at 0706, compassionate Providence sent a rain squall, under which the carriers, in conjunction with the smoke that they and the escorts were making, were protected for about fifteen minutes. During this respite the Admiral decided to bear around to the south and southwest, in order to bring his disposition nearer to the hoped-for help from Leyte Gulf. But no help appeared. Admiral Oldendorf, his ammunition depleted by the previous night's battle in Surigao Strait, had to replenish from supply ships in Leyte Gulf; and by the time he was ready to sortie it was too late to reach the flattops. Sprague's tactics were risky, since they invited the enemy to take the inside track, but they proved to be correct. Kurita was so obsessed with keeping the weather gauge that, instead of cutting corners, he maintained course until he was due north of the carriers, and then bore down. And most of his ships, repeatedly dodging air and torpedo attacks, could not catch up. The Japanese admiral was bewildered by the way everything we had afloat or airborne went baldheaded for his capital ships.

At 0716, after the escort carriers had entered the rain squall, Clifton Sprague ordered his screen to counterattack the Japanese heavy ships. His three destroyers were *Hoel,* flying the pennant of Commander W. D. Thomas, and *Heermann* and *Johnston*—all 2,100-tonners of the *Fletcher* class. *Johnston* was already counterattacking. Her skipper, Commander Ernest E. Evans, a fighting Cherokee Indian, short, barrel-chested, loud of voice, was a born leader. As soon as the Japanese ships were sighted he ordered all boilers to be lighted, called all hands to General Quarters,[1] and passed the word: "Prepare to attack major portion of Japanese Fleet." As *Johnston* sheered out to lay a smoke screen, she commenced firing at a range of 18,000 yards. Closing to within 10,000 yards of a heavy-cruiser column, she launched torpedoes and made one hit on *Kumano.* The Japanese flag officer on board shifted to *Suzuya,* which had already been slowed down by air bombing, and both cruisers dropped astern and out of the battle.

About 0730, *Johnston* took three 14-inch and three 6-inch shell hits. "It was like a puppy being smacked by a truck," recalled her senior surviving officer. The after fireroom and engine room were knocked out; all power to the after 5-inch guns was lost. A rain squall gave her ten minutes to repair damage. At this stage of the battle, confusion reigned supreme. *Johnston,* having expended all torpedoes, used manually controlled 5-inch gunfire against battleship *Kongo*; and, as if this were not enough,

[1] The sailors called *Johnston* "G.Q. Johnny," owing to her frequent General (i.e., Battle) Quarters signals.

she played the major part in frustrating Kurita's destroyer attack on the carriers. After that, said the survivor, "we were in a position where all the gallantry and guts in the world could not save us." Three cruisers and several destroyers, overtaking her when slowed down, poured in an avalanche of shells. She went dead in the water. Commander Evans ordered Abandon Ship at 0950. The same Japanese destroyer squadron whose attack on the carriers she had just thwarted, now made a running circle around her, shooting rapidly. At 1010 she rolled over and began to sink. A destroyer closed to give her the *coup de grâce*. One of her sailors, swimming, saw the Japanese skipper on her bridge salute as *Johnston* took the final plunge.

Hoel and *Heermann* were fighting just as vigorously, their skippers' one object being to inflict maximum damage on the enemy in the hope of diverting major-caliber fire from the carriers. *Heermann* (Commander A. T. Hathaway) at one point was engaging four battleships. She was too nimble for them to hit, but her spread of six torpedoes caused the mighty *Yamato* to reverse course for ten minutes, which took those 18.1-inch guns out of the fight. *Hoel* (Commander L. S. Kintberger), with one engine and three 5-inch guns knocked out, was not so lucky. She took over forty hits, even 16-inch, which went right through her hull without exploding, but knocked her so full of holes that at 0855 she rolled over and sank. Her crew, wrote her commander, "performed their duties coolly and efficiently until their ship was shot from under them."

In the second torpedo attack that Clifton Sprague

ordered, at 0742, the three destroyer escorts of his screen also took part. *Samuel B. Roberts* was sunk, after exchanging gunfire with several heavy cruisers. Here is the tribute of her skipper, Lieutenant Commander R. W. Copeland, U.S.N.R., to his men, one which may apply equally well to the entire screen:

> To witness the conduct of the average enlisted man on board this vessel . . . with an average of less than one year's service, would make any man proud to be an average American. The crew were informed over the loudspeaker system at the beginning of the action of the C.O.'s estimate of the situation: i.e., a fight against overwhelming odds from which survival could not be expected, during which time we would do what damage we could. In the face of this knowledge the men zealously manned their stations . . . and fought and worked with such calmness, courage, and efficiency that no higher honor could be conceived than to command such a group.

For two hours after 0743, when they emerged from the rain squall, the six escort carriers of Taffy 3 were making best speed of 17½ knots around an irregular arc, subtended by a chord almost parallel to the coast of Samar. Their own planes, helped by many from Taffy 2 and Taffy 1, were continually attacking the Japanese with bombs, torpedoes, and machine-gun bullets, and making "dry runs" when they ran out of ammunition. Kurita's ships were capable of twice the speed of Sprague's, but their frequent evasive maneuvers to escape torpedoes and bombing attacks canceled the advantage; while the American carriers plodded steadily along. Hence the enemy's main body never appreciably closed range. The three

Japanese battleships still advancing at 0820 were astern of the carriers, slowly firing salvos with armor-piercing projectiles which, if they hit, failed to detonate on the thin-skinned flattops. The heavy cruisers were much more deadly: they made thirteen 8-inch hits on *Kalinin Bay*, and she was the only carrier to be hit by a battleship; heroic efforts of damage control kept her in formation. Boatswains' crews worked in five feet of water to plug holes below the waterline. The "black gang" worked knee-deep in oil, choked by the stench of burning rubber and threatened by scalding steam, to repair ruptures in the power plant. Main steering control conked out and quartermasters steered the ship by hand from far down in her bowels, like helmsmen in the ancient Spanish galleons.

Aircraft for the most part made individual attacks, as they had been too hastily armed and launched to be co-ordinated. Avengers first used torpedoes, then bombs, even little 100-pounders; and when these gave out they made "dry" runs—buzzing without bombing—to divert the Japanese gunners. Lieutenant Commander Edward J. Huxtable, Air Group Commander in *Gambier Bay*, guided his Avenger for two hours through the flak to make dry runs, once flying down a line of heavy cruisers to divert them from their course and throw off their gunfire for a few precious minutes. The Wildcat pilots strafed topsides or ran interference for an Avenger; and they too made dry runs. Lieutenant Paul G. Garrison, U.S.N.R., made ten such out of a total of twenty. Since the American carriers were now scudding downwind and could not afford to luff up to recover planes, aircraft which ran out of fuel had to land on a carrier of Stump's Taffy 2 about twenty-five miles away, or on the more distant Tacloban Field, Leyte, which Army Engineers had providentially made usable. There they refueled, picked up 500-pound bombs, and flew out to sea to attack again.

The battle reached a crisis when Kurita's four remaining heavy cruisers, *Chikuma, Tone, Haguro,* and *Chokai,* more enterprising than his battlewagons, pulled ahead on the port quarter of the carriers and closed range. *Chikuma* began a steady pounding of *Gambier Bay,* from which even attacks by the intrepid *Johnston* and *Heermann* did not divert her. The escort carrier, after a salvo-chasing snake dance lasting twenty-five minutes, began to take 8-inch hits, and dropped astern. The other three heavies, light cruiser *Noshiro,* and a Japanese destroyer, concentrated on *Gambier Bay.* As she began to sink, Captain Vieweg gave the order Abandon Ship. *Chikuma* continued to pound her at short range, and at 0907 she capsized and went down.

On to the southwestward plunged the other five American flattops. *White Plains* fired her single 5-inch guns at each cruiser which closed within 18,000 yards, and made at least six hits on *Chokai.* "Hold on a little longer, boys," sang out Chief Gunner's Mate Jenkins. "We're sucking 'em into 40-mm. range!" And they almost did, or would have, but for an attack on that heavy cruiser by four Avengers led by Commander R. L. Fowler of *Kitkun Bay*'s air group. These planes scored ten hits and had the satisfaction of seeing *Chokai* go down. Next, *Chikuma* was sunk by a well co-ordinated Wildcat-

Avenger attack from Felix Stump's Taffy 2; and down she went. Clifton Sprague's harried and beset carriers, now threatened by high-caliber battleship fire as well as by *Haguro* and *Tone*, saw to their amazement both heavy cruisers break off their pursuit. A moment later a signalman on the bridge of *Fanshaw Bay* yelled: "Goddammit, boys, they're getting away!" The entire Center Force was retiring.

Kurita had ordered the break-off at 0911. The air and destroyer attacks had cost his force three heavy cruisers. His communications were so bad that he never knew how near *Tone* and *Haguro* had closed the flattops. At that time he intended merely to reassemble his dispersed and disorganized force, ascertain damage, and resume the march to Leyte Gulf. But the more he thought it over, the less he liked the prospect, and the better he relished the idea of going home the way he came. Center Force had been battered for three days—by submarines on the 23rd, fast carrier aircraft on the 24th, and in the battle just over. Kurita and his staff were so muddled as to estimate that the escort carriers were making 30 knots (instead of their maximum of 17½), so that it would be impossible to catch them. "I knew you were scared," said another admiral to Clifton Sprague after reading this postwar statement by Kurita, "but I didn't know you were *that* scared!"

Kurita had already received a radio signal from Admiral Shima indicating that Southern Force, in Surigao Strait, with which he was expected to co-operate, was all washed up. So he figured that his prospects in Leyte Gulf were both thin and grim. American transports and amphibious craft would have departed by the time he could get there; he feared massive land-based air attacks from Tacloban Field and heavy air attacks from Mitscher's fleet carriers. Nor did he care to fight Oldendorf's victorious gunfire force (which lay outside the entrance to Leyte Gulf waiting for him until 1300), in order to sink maybe a few LSTs and sprinkle shellfire on American troops ashore. A fresh air attack by 70 Wildcats and Avengers from Taffy 2 and Taffy 3, which came in on Center Force at 1230, and made hits on battleship *Nagato* and heavy cruiser *Tone*, helped Kurita to make up his mind to retire. At 1236 he signaled the Commander in Chief of the Combined Fleet at Tokyo that he was heading for San Bernardino Strait.

Kurita's retirement did not end this day's battle for the escort carriers. While Clifton Sprague's Taffy 3 was fighting to the northward, Tom Sprague's Taffy 1 was receiving the dubious honor of first target of the Kamikaze Corps, that formidable suicide club. *Santee* was crashed by a member at 0740, and hit by a torpedo from submarine *I-56* at 0756; but these converted-tanker flattops were tough, and by eight bells *Santee* was making over 16 knots. Sister *Suwannee* received a second kamikaze shortly after, but was able to resume flight operations at 1009. Taffy 3's turn came at 1050 when she hoped that the battle was over. One crashed Rear Admiral Ofstie's flagship, *Kitkun Bay*, but bounced into the sea; two that made for *Fanshaw Bay* were shot down; two were exploded by antiaircraft fire when diving at *White Plains* and *Kitkun*

Bay; two crashed *Kalinin Bay* but inflicted comparatively little damage. But one broke through the flight deck of *St. Lo*, burst into flames, exploded the bombs and torpedoes on the hangar deck, and sank her.

An hour later, Kurita's Center Force was attacked by aircraft from Admiral McCain's task group of the big fleet carriers. Admiral Halsey, at Kinkaid's urgent request, had ordered this. McCain, fueling when he got the word, turned up flank speed and commenced launching at 1030 when distant 335 miles from Kurita. This was one of the longest-range carrier plane attacks of the war; too long, for Avengers could not carry heavy bombs or torpedoes that far, and they suffered considerable loss without inflicting additional damage.

By noon the Battle off Samar was over. It had been a glorious but expensive victory: two escort carriers, two destroyers, and a destroyer escort sunk; several other ships badly damaged; and heavy casualties:

	Killed & Missing	Wounded
Taffy 1 Ships' Crews	283	136
Taffy 3 Ships' Crews	792	768
Aviators, all escort carriers	43	9
Aviators, McCain's task group	12	0
TOTAL	1,130	913

Kurita's successful retirement was small consolation for the complete failure of his mission. His defeat was due, in last analysis, to the indomitable spirit of the escort carriers, their screen, and their aviators. It was they who stopped the most powerful gunfire force which Japan had sent to sea since the Battle of Midway.

The Battle for Leyte Gulf did not end the war, but it was decisive. And it should be an imperishable part of our national memory. The night action in Surigao Strait is an inspiring example of perfect timing, co-ordination, and almost faultless execution. But the Battle off Samar had no compeer. The story of that action—with its dramatic surprise, the quick thinking and resolute decisions of Clifton Sprague; the little screening vessels feeling for each other through the rain and smoke and, courting annihilation, making individual attacks on battleships and heavy cruisers; naval aviators making dry runs on enemy ships to divert gunfire from their own; the defiant humor and indomitable courage of bluejackets caught in the "ultimate of desperate circumstances"—will make the fight of the "Taffys" with Kurita's Center Force forever memorable, forever glorious.

BIBLIOGRAPHY

Books by Samuel Eliot Morison

The Life and Letters of Harrison Gray Otis, Federalist, 1765–1848. 2 vols. Boston: Houghton Mifflin; 1913.

The Maritime History of Massachusetts. Boston: Houghton Mifflin; large paper and trade eds., 1921; rev. ed. with supplement, 1941; Sentry ed., 1961. London: Heinemann; 1923.

The Oxford History of the United States, 1783–1917. 2 vols. London and New York: Oxford University Press; 1927.

Builders of the Bay Colony. Boston: Houghton Mifflin; large paper and trade eds., 1930; Sentry ed., with supplementary chapter on William Pynchon, 1964. London: Heinemann; 1931.

The Founding of Harvard College. Cambridge, Mass.: Harvard University Press; 1935.

Harvard College in the Seventeenth Century. 2 vols. Cambridge, Mass.: Harvard University Press; 1936.

Three Centuries of Harvard. Cambridge, Mass.: Harvard University Press; 1936, 1963.

The Puritan Pronaos: Studies in the Intellectual Life of New England in the Seventeenth Century. New York: New York University Press; 1936.

The 2nd ed. is called *The Intellectual Life of Colonial New England.* New York: New York University Press; 1956. Paperback ed., Ithaca: Great Seal Books; 1960.

175

The Second Voyage of Columbus. Oxford: Clarendon Press; 1939.

Portuguese Voyages to America in the Fifteenth Century. Cambridge, Mass.: Harvard University Press; 1940.

Admiral of the Ocean Sea: A Life of Christopher Columbus. 2 vols. Boston: Atlantic–Little, Brown; 1942. 1-vol. ed., Boston: Little Brown; 1942. Paperback ed., 2 vols., New York: Time, Inc., 1962, and Mentor Books, 1962.

> Spanish trans. of 2-vol. ed., in 1 vol. *El Almirante de la Mar-Océano.* Intro. by Hector R. Ratto, Capitán de Fregata. Buenos Aires: Librería Hachette; 1943.

> German trans. of 1-vol. ed. *Admiral des Weltmeeres.* Bremen: Walter Dorn; 1948.

> French trans. of 1-vol. ed., by Josette Hesse. *Christophe Colomb, l'amiral de la mer océane.* Paris: Club des Editeurs, série Hommes et Faits de l'Histoire; n.d. Paperback ed., Paris: René Julliard; 1958.

> Portuguese trans. of 1-vol. ed., by Carlos Salvagem. *Cristóvão Colombo, Almirante do Mar-Oceano.* Lisbon: Emprêsa Nacional de Publicidade; 1962.

> Italian trans. of 1-vol. ed., by Arrigo Ballardini. *Cristoforo Colombo, ammiraglio del mare oceano.* Bologna: Società editrice il Mulino; 1962.

The Ropemakers of Plymouth. Boston: Houghton Mifflin; 1950.

By Land and By Sea. New York: Alfred A. Knopf; 1953.

The History of United States Naval Operations in World War II. 15 vols. Boston: Atlantic–Little, Brown.

> I   *The Battle of the Atlantic.* 1947; rev. ed., 1964.
> II   *Operations in North African Waters.* 1947; rev. ed., 1962.
> III *The Rising Sun in the Pacific.* 1948; rev. ed., 1963. Japanese trans., by Goro Nakano. Tokyo: Kaizo-Sha; 1949.

IV   *Coral Sea, Midway, and Submarine Actions.* 1949; rev. ed., 1962. Japanese trans., by Goro Nakano. Tokyo: Kaizo-Sha; 1950.

Partial French trans. of Vols. III and IV, by René Jouan. *Les grandes batailles navales du Pacifique, 1941–45.* Vol. I. Paris: Payot; 1949.

V   *The Struggle for Guadalcanal.* 1949; rev. ed., 1964.

French trans., by René Jouan. *Les grandes batailles navales du Pacifique, 1941–45.* Vol. II. Paris: Payot; 1952.

Spanish trans. *La Lucha por Guadalcanal.* Buenos Aires: Escuela de Guerra Naval; 1953.

VI   *Breaking the Bismarcks Barrier.* 1950; rev. ed., 1962.

Spanish trans. *Irrumpiendo en la Barrera de las Bismarck.* Buenos Aires: Escuela de Guerra Naval; 1954.

VII   *Aleutians, Gilberts, and Marshalls.* 1951; rev. ed., 1962.

VIII   *New Guinea and the Marianas.* 1953; rev. ed., 1962.

IX   *Sicily—Salerno—Anzio.* 1954; rev. ed., 1964.

X   *The Atlantic Battle Won.* 1956; rev. ed., 1964.

XI   *The Invasion of France and Germany.* 1957; rev. ed., 1964. Russian trans., Moscow; 1963.

XII   *Leyte, June 1944–January 1945.* 1958; rev. ed., 1963.

Partial trans. of Vols. VIII and XII, by René Jouan. *Les grandes batailles navales du Pacifique, 1941–45.* Vol. III: *La bataille de la mer des Philippines, la bataille de Leyte.* Paris: Payot; 1959.

XIII   *The Liberation of the Philippines.* 1963.

XIV   *Victory in the Pacific.* 1961.

XV   *Supplement and General Index.* 1962.

Christopher Columbus, Mariner. Boston: Atlantic–Little, Brown; 1955.

British ed., enlarged and with illustrations. London: Faber & Faber; 1955.

Paperback ed. New York: Mentor Books; 1956.

Paperback "Ladder ed. at the 1000-Word Level," with notes in Japanese. Tokyo: Kaitakusha; 1963.

Italian trans., by Attilio Landi. *Cristoforo Colombo.* Milan: Arnoldo Mondadori; 1958.

Dutch trans., by G. H. H. Schröder. *Columbus de zeevarder.* Utrecht: Vitgeverij Spectrum; n.d.

Hungarian trans., by Neményi Ödön. *Kolumbusz Kristóf a Tengerész.* Budapest: Gondolat; 1959.

Polish trans., by Bronislaw Wojciechowski. *Krzysztof Kolumb.* Warsaw: Iskry; 1963.

Russian trans. *Christophor Kolum.* Moscow; 1958.

Persian trans., by Mohammad Saeedi. Teheran: Amirkabir; 1959.

Arabic trans., by Fawzi Kiblawi. Beirut: Dar Maktabat Al-Hayat; 1959.

Freedom in Contemporary Society. Boston: Atlantic–Little, Brown; 1956.

Portuguese trans., by Ubaldo Bezerra Nero. *A Liberdade na sociedade contemporânea.* Rio de Janeiro: Editoro Fundo de Cultura; 1959.

Korean trans., by Geuk-chan Lee. Seoul: Eul-Yoo; 1958.

The Story of the "Old Colony" of New Plymouth, 1620–1692. New York: Alfred A. Knopf; 1956.

Strategy and Compromise. Boston: Atlantic–Little, Brown, 1958.

The British ed. is called: *American Contributions to Strategy of World War II.* London: Faber & Faber; 1958.

John Paul Jones: A Sailor's Biography. Boston: Atlantic–Little, Brown, 1959; also in paperback. London: Faber & Faber; 1959.

Spanish trans. *John Paul Jones.* Madrid: Plaza & Janés SA; 1962.

The Story of Mount Desert Island, Maine. Boston: Atlantic–Little, Brown; 1960.

One Boy's Boston, 1887–1901. Boston: Houghton Mifflin; 1962.

The Two-Ocean War, a Short History of the U. S. Navy in the Second World War. Boston: Atlantic–Little, Brown; 1963.

Vistas of History. New York: Alfred A. Knopf; 1964.

In Preparation

With Mauricio Obregon: *The Caribbean as Columbus Saw It.* Boston: Atlantic–Little, Brown.

The Oxford History of the American People. New York: Oxford University Press.

Spring Tides: Essays on the Sea and Seafaring. Boston: Houghton Mifflin.

The Life of Commodore Matthew Calbraith Perry. Boston: Atlantic–Little, Brown.

With Henry Steele Commager

The Growth of the American Republic. 1 vol. New York: Oxford University Press; 1930, 1936; 2nd ed., 2 vols., 1937; 3rd ed., 2 vols., 1942; 4th ed., 2 vols., 1950; 5th ed., 2 vols., 1962.

German trans. *Das Werden der Amerikanischen Republik.* Stuttgart: Deutsche Verlags-Anhalt; 1950.

Portuguese trans., by Agenor Soares de Moura. *História dos Estados Unidos do América*. São Paulo: Edições Melhoramentos; n.d.

Spanish trans., by Odón Durán d'Ocón and Faustino Ballvé. *Historia de los Estados Unidos de Norteamérica*. 3 vols. Mexico City: Fondo de Cultura Económica; 1951.

Italian trans., by Clementina Arangio-Ruiz Ardito. *Storia degli Stati Uniti d'America*. 2 vols. Florence: La Nuova Italia; 1960.

Books Edited by Samuel Eliot Morison

The Key of Libberty [sic], *Written in the year 1798 by William Manning*. Billerica, Mass.: The Manning Association; 1922. Reprinted in *William and Mary Quarterly*, 3rd Series, XIII (1956), 202–54.

Sources and Documents Illustrating the American Revolution and Formation of the Federal Constitution. Oxford: Clarendon Press; 1923. Rev. eds. to 1960.

The Development of Harvard University, 1869–1929. Cambridge, Mass.: Harvard University Press; 1929.

With Zechariah Chafee, Jr.: *Records of the Suffolk County Court, 1671–1680*. *Publications of the Colonial Society of Massachusetts*, XXIX, XXX (1933).

The Log Cabin Myth, a Study of the Early Dwellings of the English Colonists in North America, by Harold R. Shurtleff. Cambridge, Mass.: Harvard University Press; 1939.

Of Plymouth Plantation, by William Bradford. New York: Alfred A. Knopf; 1952. Parts reprinted in *Major Writers of America*. New York: Harcourt, Brace and World; 1963.

BIBLIOGRAPHY

The Parkman Reader. Boston: Atlantic–Little, Brown; 1955.
The British ed. is called: *France and England in North America.* London: Faber & Faber; 1955.

History of the Conquest of Peru, by William H. Prescott. New York: Limited Editions Club, de luxe ed., 1957; Heritage Press ed., 1957.

Journals and Other Documents on the Life and Voyages of Christopher Columbus. New York: Limited Editions Club, de luxe ed., 1963; Heritage Press ed., 1964.

A Note on the Type

The text of this book is set in *Caledonia,* a Linotype face designed by W. A. Dwiggins, the man responsible for so much that is good in contemporary book design and typography. Caledonia belongs to the family of printing types called "modern face" by printers—a term used to mark the change in style of type-letters that occurred about 1800. Caledonia borders on the general design of Scotch Modern but is more freely drawn than that letter.

Composed, printed, and bound by
The Haddon Craftsmen, Scranton, Pa.
Typography and binding design based on
originals by W. A. Dwiggins